W9-AEF-227

THE OLD TESTAMENT AND OUR TIMES

A Short Reading Course with Subjects for Discussion

The Old Testament and Our Times

A Short Reading Course with Subjects for discussion

MARGARET T. MONRO

LONGMANS

LONGMANS, GREEN AND CO LTD
6 & 7 CLIFFORD STREET, LONDON W1
THIBAULT HOUSE, THIBAULT SQUARE, CAPE TOWN
605–611 LONSDALE STREET, MELBOURNE C1
443 LOCKHART ROAD, HONG KONG
ACCRA, AUCKLAND, IBADAN
KINGSTON (JAMAICA), KUALA LUMPUR
LAHORE, NAIROBI, SALISBURY (RHODESIA)
LONGMANS, GREEN AND CO INC
119 WEST 40TH STREET, NEW YORK 18
LONGMANS, GREEN AND CO
20 CRANFIELD ROAD, TORONTO 16
ORIENT LONGMANS PRIVATE LTD
CALCUTTA, BOMBAY, MADRAS
DELHI, HYDERABAD, DACCA

First Published 1960

IMPRIMATUR

NIHIL OBSTAT JOANNES M. T. BARTON, S.T.D., L.S.S., CENSOR DEPUTATUS. IMPRIMATUR E. MORROGH BERNARD, VIC., GEN., WESTMONASTERII, DIE 16 JULII, 1960. THE NIHIL OBSTAT AND IMPRIMATUR ARE A DECLARATION THAT A BOOK OR PAMPHLET IS CONSIDERED TO BE FREE FROM DOCTRINAL OR MORAL ERROR. IT IS NOT IMPLIED THAT THOSE WHO HAVE GRANTED THE NIHIL OBSTAT AND IMPRIMATUR AGREE WITH THE CONTENTS OPINIONS OR STATEMENTS EXPRESSED.

Contents

Preface

THIS LITTLE BOOK began as a series of articles contributed during 1959 to *The Mercat Cross*, published in Edinburgh by the Jesuit Fathers, to whom I tender warm thanks for the readiness to let them appear in book form. Expansions and alterations however are few, just enough to make the difference between magazine articles and a book.

Like the articles, the book is offered to those who come new to the Old Testament. Since the object is to whet interest, there is a not a systematic course of reading so much as a set of samples to awaken a desire to go further. These samples have been chosen for their bearing on issues that confront us to-day. At first sight it may seem strange that a book as ancient as the Old Testament should have anything to offer to our chaotic century; yet such is the discovery of those who venture on the voyage of exploration. The evidence that God has before now guided the world through desperate crises is of course heartening. But there is more—concrete help in facing the crises of our own times, if only in learning to think and speak of them in a way that 'touches the spot' with our bewildered contemporaries.

Because the book is meant thus as a start and no more, it has seemed best to begin with what is nearest to us in time, perhaps closer in kinship to our own ways of thinking, and then to work backwards. We start with the Wisdom Movement, then do some rather haphazard exploring among the Prophets, notably their protest against the social and economic evils of their times. It was Isaias who gave us the phrase, now unfortunately hackneyed, about 'grinding the faces of the poor'. (Think of it in terms of the old-fashioned handmill and see if it does not come alive.) We then take a look at the way a new metal, iron, altered the character of war and industry, and among other things altered the character of the Jewish monarchy. Passages from the Historical Books are included to make clear the points raised.

The last two chapters are more general. The one deals with the changing world-picture which Christians in different ages have had to accept from the science of their times, beginning with the earliest of all, that taken for granted in the Old Testament. The final chapter then deals with the life after death; it is remarkable how the Old Testament approach clarifies much that is troubling our contemporaries to-day.

Put somewhat differently, this choice of present-day issues is not decided by academic considerations but by the highly practical business of our apostolate to our contemporaries. A Catholic can hardly help being an apostle; his only choice is to be a clumsy or a competent one. The post-Christian world is much closer to the pre-Christian than is generally recognised. The Old Testament helps us in two ways; it enables us to see these perennial issues more clearly, in a larger setting; and it enriches and broadens our powers of sympathy. A chance encounter, in railway carriage or through holiday contacts, may well leave a Catholic thanking God that he has something more than a devotional acquaintance with the Old Testament.

MARGARET T. MONRO

Feast of the Ascension, 1959

INTRODUCTION

Some Things to Remember About the Old Testament

OUR GREATEST difficulty with the Old Testament is that it comes to us from a civilisation from which our own is not descended. From the world of the New Testament, we inherit not only our religion, but a living tradition that includes government, law, literature, learning, philosophy, science, the arts, and even manners. From the Old Testament period our sole inheritance is our religion.

Further, the Church has for the most part transformed that heritage into forms contemporary with ourselves. We do not normally need to delve into the past in order to enter upon this religious inheritance. The great truths of the Old Testament, and much of its noblest poetry, are mediated to us in our prayers, notably in the Mass and the Divine Office, while almost any instruction draws, even unwittingly, on what the Old Testament has to tell us about God and His relations with man.

The easy way round this difficulty is to remember the following points.

1. The Old Testament is the story of an education. It tells how God took a very ordinary sample of humanity, below rather than above its contemporaries in culture, and trained that people until it became the seed-bed of His final revelation.

2. God did not make things easy for Himself. Not only was the chosen people a tough subject for education; it had about the worst possible environment. Western Asia was the region in which human religion had become more horribly corrupted than anywhere else in the world. In the face of abominations such as the sacrifice of children to Moloch, and the foul rite of religious prostitution, God 'put across' the truths which we to-

day class as Natural Religion. This mighty truth prevailed, not where conditions were easiest but where they were hardest.

3. Another difficulty was that the homeland of the Jews was anything but a sheltered nook. It was a sort of bridge between the great powers on the Nile to the south-west, and the Tigris and Euphrates to the north-east, a through road for both trade and war. Armies constantly trampled back and forth; the Jews were as corn between the upper and lower millstones. This fact was used by God to discipline them at last into obedience to Himself. After the Exile in Babylon there was no more idolatry.

4. Hence there is in the Old Testament a marked element of growth. We are accustomed to the idea that the New Testament is an advance on the Old. Actually the later parts of the Old Testament are an almost greater advance on some elements in the earlier parts. While God at first tolerated many imperfect notions, as with divorce, the general effect was to make it possible for His people to outgrow those imperfect notions.

5. Here is a somewhat startling sample. One of the first lessons God had to drive home was that He was in full control of all that happens. And until His people had a firm grip on this, He did not bother them with details they were not yet ready to digest. Hence we find Old Testament writers speaking as if God were the doer of evil. Amos for instance is found saying, as part of an argument, 'Shall there be evil in a city, which the Lord hath not done?' (Am. 3: 6). The context shows that evil here means rather misfortune, punishment for the people's wrong-doing. Even so, the phrase is startling. Only by degrees did God lead His people to see that wills other than His own played a part in deciding the course of events, finite wills, whether of angels, good or bad, or of men. . . . This, of course, is a sample of good teaching method. One would hardly expect God to be an incompetent teacher!

6. Because of this educational factor, there is much in the Old Testament which is not, in the superficial sense, edifying. But in a more fundamental sense it builds us up, which is what 'edifies' really means. This upbuilding works through training our judgment, sometimes on definitely difficult and puzzling

material. Its chief result is to open our eyes to the fact that if God did not concern Himself with evil-doers He would not be the Father perfect in love whom we know through Christ. No one is too bad or too stupid or too undeveloped or too muddle-headed or too weak to matter to God. That is a very 'edifying' truth to get a hold on.

7. The Old Testament never flatters even its great and good men. It is completely frank about the failures and weaknesses of those who were, in our phrase, 'on the side of the angels'. There are delightful people in the Old Testament whose memory we rightly revere. Yet not one single one of them is presented as faultless. This integrity of the Old Testament historians is a great virtue.

And in some cases where perhaps the sacred writer does not fully see the moral standards which Christians take for granted, the Holy Ghost, by inspiring him to such accuracy, indirectly gives a hint of where the trouble lies. For instance, nowhere in the Old Testament is polygamy condemned. But in the two full-length pictures of a polygamous family, the sons of Jacob in Genesis and the sons of David in Kings, the effect is so hideous as to amount to moral condemnation.

8. The moral condemnation is often oblique, and lies in the way the story is told, the results that flow from this or that action—for instance, the way David's sensuality led to the rebellions of the end of his reign.

9. The Old Testament was written in days when writing materials were very, very costly. A writer could not spare precious space for anything that did not absolutely need to be said. He had to trust the commonsense and co-operation of his readers even more than a writer has to do to-day. Hence he rarely wasted expensive writing materials on saying whether an action was good or bad; he expected the reader to be able to see that for himself. So be sure to take your commonsense with you when you read the Old Testament, for its authors are counting on your bringing it along.

10. The Old Testament always makes evil shocking, a rarer feat than may at first be realized. It is fatally easy to make it

attractive or not worth worrying about. The mere fact that in places we are shocked is a testimony to the moral quality in the writing.

LITERARY CONVENTIONS

Every book in the Old Testament has to be judged according to its own literary kind. We can all see that it is silly to judge poetry as if it were prose. There is a great deal of poetry in the Old Testament, and the Hebrew poets, like those of all other lands, dealt in metaphors which are not meant to be taken literally. Understood rightly, as metaphors, they open up great fields of truth.

As to the kinds of literature—it is probable, though not certain, that the Canticle is a work of fiction (other aspects will be touched on when it is proposed for reading). Then, some stories such as Tobias, Esther and Judith, and to some degree Jonas, may have been worked up from earlier records whether oral or written; in that case, the moralising belongs to the age in which they were re-cast; the point and purpose of the tale is later than the time when the events occurred.

There are many short dramatic passages in the Old Testament in which it is necessary to distinguish who is talking, but only one book is wholly drama, Job. In order to bring his argument alive the author has put the various sides of the case in the mouths of different characters. Hence it will not do to take a verse at random from Job (or any other dramatic passage) and say: 'This is in the Bible, it must be true.' It may be one of the things of which God says, 'Who is this that wrappeth up sentences in unskilful words?' (Job 38: 1). As a more extreme example, the Bible does contain the sentence, 'There is no God'; but it is ushered in with, 'The fool hath said in his heart' (Ps. 13: 1.).

More puzzling than these points is a literary convention called *pseudepigraphy*. We should consider it dishonest for a writer to attribute his work to a great man of the past. The Jews thought it a piece of praiseworthy modesty. What started it was that in two cases a great man founded a collection which was further developed. David made the first collection of songs for use in the worship of the Temple and contributed his own poems to it; Solomon similarly made the first collection of Proverbs. In either case, good work worthy to stand beside the original collection was later incorporated. Hence by degrees the name 'David' came to be associated with all psalmody, while the name 'Solomon' came to mean 'work in the style which Solomon introduced'. Thus the Canticle is called 'of Solomon' and the Book of Wisdom is treated as if the speaker all through were Solomon himself; in either case it was the writer's way of telling his readers the *kind* of work he was attempting. Another writer to whom similar attributions were made is Daniel; many scholars now think that the visionary section (Daniel, chaps. 7–12) was written in a style begun by Daniel, by a writer of the Macchabaean period with which these visions deal. Actually, pseudepigraphy hardly concerns us in this book save as it touches the styles inaugurated by David and Solomon.

HINTS ON USING THIS BOOK

If possible, read from the Knox Version. Quotations in this book are made from the Douay, but the Knox is often much easier to understand.

Take seriously the sections *For Reading*: after all, the book has been written for their sakes.

The sections *For Discussion* are primarily meant for study groups, but they have been handled in the hope of being useful also to lone readers.

Keep an atlas handy. One with good maps of the Near East would do. But a real Bible Atlas, whether Catholic or Protestant, would be better. The great Catholic *Atlas of the Bible*, by Grollenberg (English translation published by Thos. Nelson & Sons at 70s.) might be found in a public library or would be got on request. This is also now available in a smaller edition, *A Shorter Atlas of the Bible*, at 15s.

Even better maps are to be found in *The Westminster Atlas of the Bible*, by a group of American Protestant scholars. It is called after the city of Westminster in the United States, and has nothing to do with the Catholic Westminster Version of the Bible. It also has an admirable shorter edition, containing maps only, *The Westminster Smaller Bible Atlas*, costing only 4s. 6d., Both the "Westminster" Atlases are published in Great Britain by the Student Christian Movement Press.

CHAPTER ONE

The Wisdom Movement in General

As INDICATED in the Preface, we are going to let ourselves down gently by starting with those parts of the Old Testament which are nearest to ourselves, least foreign and unfamiliar. Instead of starting with the remote beginnings of God's dealings with our race, we shall look first at a comparatively late development, and from that work backwards into increasingly foreign territory with (let us hope) increasing enjoyment of our adventure.

This late development is called the Wisdom Movement, which was carried forward by a special class known as Wise Men. Two other groups were entitled to teach God's people: the priests who expounded the Law of Moses, and the prophets who spoke directly for God when His chosen people needed fresh light on their path. Both priest and prophet, though in different ways, took their start from God's revelation.

It is remarkable therefore to find a parallel movement which did not start thus with God speaking but with men thinking. Without being exactly rationalistic, the Wisdom Movement was an attempt to apply the human understanding to the issues of life. Above all, there was a close study of conduct, and alongside it a contemplation of nature, the two fields in which the mind—in Hebrew idiom the 'heart'—could most readily discern God at work.

This point about idiom should be noted. With us, the heart is the seat of the emotions. In Hebrew it is frequently the seat of the understanding, the emotions being associated with the bowels. An instance is the phrase 'bowels of compassion' (Ps. 24: 6, echoed several times in the New Testament, e.g., 1 John 3: 17; Phil. 1: 8; 2: 1; Col. 3: 12). In the Old Testament, we do well to pause on meeting the word 'heart', to see whether the passage favours an emotional or an intellectual sense. For the latter, see for instance Job 9: 4; 38: 36; Prov. 10: 8.

Yet it is a special kind of understanding, not the intellect working alone, but rather a response of the whole man, led indeed by his intelligence, but also drawing on imagination, conscience and right feeling.

THE QUEST FOR WISDOM

This quest for Wisdom did not begin in Israel. It arose in the surrounding lands, Egypt, Babylonia, to a lesser degree Assyria, and also among the small nations near at hand across the Jordan. The Book of Proverbs contains two short sections from a Transjordan people called the Massaites, who were not Israelites but descended from Abraham's son Ismael.

The Edomites, descended from Jacob's twin brother Esau, later Israel's most persistent foes, were also addicted to the study of Wisdom. Jeremias (49: 7) mentions the Edomite town of Theman as a centre for the study of Wisdom. The author of the Book of Job, who knew Edom well and seems to have liked the Edomites, since he chose his hero from among them, calls one of Job's friends Eliphaz the Themanite. Is this a hint as to where the great poet who gave us this great book made his own studies in Wisdom?

To get at the start of the movement, we need to look at the ancient cultures as a group, notably those that arose in the great river valleys, the Nile, the Euphrates and Tigris, the Indus, the Ganges, the Yangtse and the Hoang-ho. For all their local differences, the early history of these cultures is markedly similar, not least in the way religion and morality were closely associated as in the Mosaic Law.

This was not always to the advantage of morality. Where men worship bad gods, or even incomplete gods, morality has something to lose as well as to gain by close association with religion. Fortunately, in conscience there is always a possible mainspring of revolt. Hence in course of time, the more serious spirits in many lands began a study of conduct as something distinct from the traditional ideas associated with religion.

At first at any rate the object seems to have been purely practical. 'What', this new class of Wise Men asked, 'is the best way to ensure a happy lifetime? What should we avoid, what should we practise, in order to enjoy the best that a lifetime has to offer?'

Wisdom thus conceived ranged wide. On one side it concerned itself with manners, marriage, how to get on with other people, hard work in order to avoid want, respectful attention to those who had more experience of life and its difficulties. On another side, it is concerned with government and the conduct of affairs. Only in Greece does there seem to have been an attempt to work out a genuine philosophy of right and wrong.

Obviously, much that the Wise Men of all lands had to say was addressed to those embarking on the voyage of life. Wisdom is predominantly aimed at the young. Taking their start from popular proverbs, the Wise Men developed a medium for expressing their observations on the conduct of life: close-wrought, pithy statements, easily remembered for their witty turn or for a striking or amusing illustration. 'A golden ring in a swine's snout, a woman fair and foolish'—the first hearers surely sniggered (Prov. 11: 22).

Indeed, the proverb was often a miniature parable. 'Go to the ant, O sluggard, and consider her ways and learn wisdom', is a good sample of the new medium (Prov. 6: 6).

THE INFLUENCE OF SURROUNDING NATIONS

On one point Jewish tradition is unanimous: it was Solomon who introduced this new study or pastime—it was a bit of both—to his subjects. The nucleus of the Book of Proverbs was compiled by him or under his auspices, later collections being added when judged fit to stand beside his.

The little account in 3 Kings 4: 29–34 makes it clear that Solomon's interest in plants and animals was as material for these parable-proverbs. Moreover, verse 31 shows awareness that he was taking up a *genre* already cultivated elsewhere. But the author of this section of Kings does not mention what may have been his most interesting source of inspiration, an Egyptian work, *The Teaching of Amen-em-ope*, (Amenophis in Greek). This is so close to part of Proverbs that one of them must have influenced the other, and scholars consider it more likely to have been Egypt that wielded the influence.

As to when this happened, there is not yet complete agreement, chiefly because the Egyptologists vary widely in their dating of the work. The suggested dates run from 1000 B.C. to 600 B.C. If the earliest dating is correct, it could have been known to Solomon, who reigned from about 972–931 B.C. Through Solomon's marriage with an Egyptian princess, Egyptian cultural influence was strong in Palestine in his time.

If, however, Amen-em-ope lived later than Solomon, the only other period when Jews would have had an opportunity to study his work was after 586 B.C., the year in which Nabuchodonosor destroyed Jerusalem and deported most of the Jews to Babylon. A minority, however, escaped to Egypt, where their descendants remained even after Cyrus the Great of Persia allowed the Jewish deportees to return to their own land (538 B.C. onwards). The Jewish community in Egypt adopted the Greek language, especially in Alexandria, and became of great cultural importance through its contacts with both Egyptian and Hellenic learning.

If this later date is correct, then the section influenced by Amen-em-ope is a sample of the way Solomon's nucleus was later expanded to include collections judged fit to stand by his, as was explained in the section on Literary Conventions in the Introduction (pp. 4–5).

This is not the only case in which Jewish writers concerned with morals were influenced by work done in other lands; details are given in the section For Reading below. The fact is worth pondering. The Wisdom Movement was the point at which the Chosen People were in closest contact with their neighbours, least affected by the barriers erected by the Law. Their recognition that even pagans might produce thoughts on morals with which the Law of God had no quarrel is striking. Indeed, more is in the picture than Israel's immediate neighbours. Far over the horizons of Israel, the sages of India and China were doing the same sort of thing through approximately the same centuries. God did not miraculously make His people aware of that more distant work. But the inclusion of some instances of the noblest pagan work in inspired Scripture allows us to feel God's hand laid in blessing on the whole of this far-flung attempt to establish the rules of right conduct.

A DIFFERENCE

Yet with all the likenesses we must note a difference, one we shall constantly find cropping up in connection with the Old Testament: in all sorts of ways, the Jews began much where other peoples did, then went somewhere quite different. As Our Lord indicated, it is by the fruits rather than the roots that we should judge a plant.

The Wisdom Movement is a striking instance of the way in which a root found in many lands produced in Israel a fruit found nowhere else. In many countries, the effect of this new study of conduct was to widen the gap between the religionists and the moralists. The reason was that the gods of those countries were impossible to link up with any serious kind of morality. In Israel alone, the effect of the study of Wisdom was to bring the students of virtue back to God, with a freshened realisation of His goodness and truth.

That is why the Jewish Wise Men are so enraptured by the Law. It was a manifestation of the Divine Wisdom at least as great as its manifestation in nature, their other favourite theme. Nor did their quest for Wisdom stop at the Law or the Wonders of Creation. In either case, they found they had to go further. The Law and Nature were spheres of Wisdom, not its origin. To find the origin of Wisdom they had to plunge deeper. Their quest thus led them to a profound realisation of the true and only source of all Wisdom: God Himself. No other people made that particular journey.

FOR READING

Besides looking up all the references given in the course of the chapter, try these:

1. *Links with Other Lands.* Prov. 22: 17–24: 22, where the similarity to Amen-em-ope is closest.

Prov. 30: 1–14 and 31: 1–9, from the Ismaelite kingdom of Massa.

Prov. 30: 15b–33. These 'threes and fours' are close to some tablets found in the temple library of Ugarit, a city excavated near Ras Shamra in Syria (1929–38, resumed in 1948).

Job 31, called his 'negative confession', not unlike a section of the Egyptian *Book of the Dead,* in which the soul of the dead man protests to the gods of the underworld that he had not committed a number of evil acts, much in the vein of Job.

Ps. 103. This is perhaps not quite in line with the Wisdom Movement, though akin. A Jew in Egypt, during or after the Exile in Babylon, seems to have come across an Egyptian poem at least eight hundred years old by then, the 'Hymn of the Sun' composed by the Pharaoh Akhen-Aten. This remarkable man, worth a hundred of his son-in-law Tut-Ankh-Amen, whose unrifled tomb made such a stir between the wars, had tried to found a monotheistic religion with the sun's disc as its symbol for deity. Fortunately the Jew in Egypt was a poet. Stirred by the ancient hymn, he tried his hand at something similar and gave us this great Creation Psalm.

2. *Contemplation of Nature.* Job 28. This delightful account of the mining for gems and ores for which Edom was famous is generally regarded as an insertion breaking the thread of a speech by Job.

Job 26: 7–14 is regarded by some scholars as a speech by Baldad the Suhite copied by accident into a speech by Job; it is much more Baldad's line of country.

Prov. 8, where the speaker is Wisdom personified. Baruch 3: 9–38; Ecclus. 24 and 43.

3. *Some 'Wisdom' Psalms.* Psalm 18. The first seven verses are an archaic nature-poem to which a Wisdom writer, using Hebrew of a later period, has added a stanza on the Law as God's light on earth, parallel to the sun in the sky.

Ps. 24, 33 and 36 are all acrostics on the Hebrew alphabet, a device to which the Wisdom[1] writers were much attached. (See for

[1] 'Of David' in the title here means either 'about David' or 'the kind of thing David would have said'.

instance the poem with which Ecclesiasticus ends; the Knox version brings out the acrostic character of these passages.)

Ps. 118 is a full-length treatment, still acrostic in pattern, of the Law as the supreme manifestation of God's wisdom on earth.

FOR DISCUSSION

The obvious point would seem to be the relation of religion and morals, which is much debated to-day.

1. Whether religion is good for morals depends on the kind of god worshipped. Bacchus for instance was worshipped by getting drunk.

2. Even a religion with a good god may be adduced as an excuse for actions otherwise accounted wicked.

3. Generally speaking, so long as a religion is taken seriously the moral code connected with it is liable to be fairly well obeyed. If the religion wanes the moral code may wane with it—not invariably a bad thing!

4. Without religion, morality becomes something cold and cheerless. It is taken out of the sphere of the masses to become the private preserve of a minority of the well-to-do who have a bias towards respectability. Two sets of people are then left out in the cold. First, the multitude, so often pushed into wrong-doing by sheer pressure of circumstances. And second, those of the well-to-do who find virtue a bore and merely want their fun.

5. It seems to take a religion to give morality sanctions that can be appreciated by the common run of mortals.

6. Those who claim that morality can stand without religion are apt to find themselves in difficulties when their children start saying, 'But why shouldn't I . . . ?'

7. Perhaps the most important thing is to avoid taking for granted a close association between religion and morality everywhere and at all periods. In the more self-conscious periods which come later in the history of all cultures, only Judaism and Christianity have kept that association going over long periods of time, and they have not always found it easy. We are of course used to the association; hence we are apt to say 'natural' when we mean 'familiar', and 'normal' when we mean 'traditional among ourselves'.

One of our best helps towards meeting the challenge now openly made to that traditional association is to realise that we defend—still more exemplify—something not too easy to parallel.

CHAPTER TWO

The Wisdom Movement: An Education for Boys

THERE ARE three main strands in the Wisdom Books that have come down to us. First is the practical task of preparing young people to order their lives well. This takes the form both of moral counsels and of studies of great examples from the past. Second comes the contemplation of nature as a manifestation of the Divine Wisdom, closely linked with the Law as a similar sphere in which the orderly Wisdom of God can be discerned in action.

The third strand is not meant for the young. It is the Wise Men's own, adult, reaction to the plain fact that human affairs do not always afford an obvious illustration of the Divine Wisdom. This challenge of the actual is felt by the Wise Men in many forms and from many directions; but the focal point is the suffering of the innocent. Here, thought was held up for centuries because the Jews had confused and inadequate ideas on the life after death.

THE AFTER-LIFE

It can be a shock to realise, for the first time, how much of the Old Testament was written without any clear view of a moral character in the life after death. This is one of the most important points at which the Jews started where many other peoples did, then went somewhere different, because they followed original and unusual roads. While a full treatment of this important theme must wait for our last chapter, a brief outline is here needed if we are to have a background for our reading.

In a general way, the life after death is something about which men can spell out a good deal by the use of their reason and conscience. Yet in actual fact they hardly ever do. In ancient times, the Egyptians were ahead of their contemporaries in seeing that men's conduct on earth affected their fate after death. Yet even they mixed up this genuine insight with a lot of rubbishy superstitions and some very serious misinterpretations. This may be why God shielded the Chosen People from being influenced by the real greatness of Egyptian thought on this subject. Even after spending a couple of centuries in Egypt, before their Exodus under the leadership of Moses, the Jews still clung to a much inferior view which their ancestors had brought from Mesopotamia.

In that inferior view, at death the ghosts descended to an underground region called Sheol, where they endured an existence of incredible dreariness. In Sheol, all were on a footing of equality, not least in the fact that nothing interesting could ever happen to them again. As long as this defective view held the field, no great progress could be made with the problem of innocent suffering.

And at first sight God's treatment of His Chosen People seems utterly odd: He gave them almost no direct help in this quest. Prophets protested to Him, and were braced up, sometimes quite sharply. God's help was not given by relieving His servants of the labour of using their own minds; it was given rather through painful experiences which forced them to think hard in order to penetrate to anything like sense. In practice, this meant that, though some prophets did excellent work on the problem, in the main it was taken out of their hands and passed over to the Wise Men. This was because the prophets depended on a word from God (which in the matter of the after-life God was not going to utter), while the function of the Wise Men was to approach such issues from the side of human reason. Hence it comes that, in spite of noble contributions from some prophets—chiefly perhaps through their suffering lives—it was the Wise Men who first worked out anything like a complete outline of an answer. Their significance is not exhausted by their work for the immature, though it was that which people in general most noticed and commended.

THE WISDOM BOOKS OF THE OLD TESTAMENT

Here then is a brief survey of the Wisdom Books:

Proverbs, in nucleus at least the earliest, is mainly concerned with the training of the young, along with the intertwined theme of God's work in creation.

Job is wholly given over to the question of the Innocent Sufferer, and offers the first theory that successfully breached the old position that suffering is always deserved. The new theory is that it could be in some cases a test—the first crack in the old heart-crushing view that we invariably deserve exactly what happens to us. In some quarters (Tobias 2: 10–18) the new theory was received with enthusiasm. But the author of Ecclesiastes seems to have heard of it but does not make it his own; he seems rather to feel that our life on earth is too great a muddle to fit any theory (3: 18–19). It is always interesting to note instances in which different Biblical authors take different views of the same ideas or events, through seeing them in a different context: thus all sides of truth are gradually brought out.

Ecclesiastes seems to be a collection of jottings, made on and off in the course of a lifetime, and dealing with what George MacDonald, a century ago, called 'the God-denying look of things'. Its author, commonly referred to as the Ecclesiast, was apparently a teacher of the young, some of whose 'proverbs' became deservedly famous, chapter 12 in particular. In these jottings we get the story of his inner life, set down haphazard through the years. From them we gather that he had begun in youth with high hopes from the study of Wisdom, then turned against it feeling it had let him down; this human quest did not answer the cry of his heart. But after trying pleasure and business, he found them even more disappointing. Above all, his old longing for light on the puzzle of life re-awakened, and brought him back to Wisdom, his first love, as the least disappointing thing within his reach. He is a pessimist and a man of markedly unconventional outlook, with a strict integrity which refused to accept cheap consolations and easy answers.

In the end he got some light on his worries, but like other Jews in similar case he had to realise that the only real answer is God Himself.

Ecclesiasticus by contrast is primarily a handbook for the instruction of the young, but that instruction included some of the most inspiring passages we have on the Divine Wisdom, especially as manifested in nature. The author, Ben Sirach, deliberately uses these to encourage the student to stick to his rather boring task of memorising.

The Book of Wisdom, by an anonymous author who puts all he has to say in the mouth of Solomon, was probably composed in Egypt, and in Greek, not Hebrew or Aramaic. It carries the twin themes of the life after death and the innocent sufferer as far as they could be carried before the Incarnation. Though it does not neglect the needs of young students, especially through reflections on the great men of old, its main importance is on the side of meeting the challenge which life offers to those who worship the One Good God. After all, worshippers of bad gods have no problem of evil—how should they? The book is one of the glories of human reason working on the data of human experience. It is also a reminder, unintentionally, that something more is needed if those great gains are to be securely held.

Canticles will be considered at the end of the next chapter. There are also a number of 'Wisdom' passages scattered through later books of the Old Testament—Baruch, Tobias, Judith and so forth.

EDUCATION

From the start, the Wisdom Movement had been concerned with showing young people how to live a full and happy life. To this end the parable-proverb had been developed, as something easy to remember. For, at first at least, this new type of education did not necessarily involve reading and writing. It was imparted by mouth and acquired by ear.

It can be startling to realise that the great men of antiquity—whole dynasties of Pharaohs and kings of Babylon, let alone kings of Israel and Juda—were illiterate but not therefore uneducated. Ancient systems of writing were clumsy and elaborate, valued for decoration as much as for utility, and to a large extent the private preserve of a profession or trade. A great king like Hammurabi of Babylon, whose Code of Laws may have influenced Moses, or the Pharaoh Akhen Aten whose Hymn of the Sun we considered in the last chapter, felt no more inferiority in employing someone to do his reading and writing for him than we do in employing a doctor to tell us how to keep well. There was no loss of prestige for anyone in the fact that he needed the services of a trained expert.

All the same, there is something about writing not quite on a level with other trades and professions. Those who practised it came to fill positions of trust, as accountants and auditors as well as scribes. In some cases the professional reader and writer became the Secretary of State, the chief prize of the profession. When easier scripts were invented, so that more people could write their own letters and keep their own accounts, the scribes took over the work we should now call editing, printing and publishing. While the Wise Men were not identical with the scribes, and did not teach reading and writing, a time came when their pupils came to them already knowing how to read, and that to some extent altered the character of the Wise Men's books. Yet to the end they were remembered and praised for their skill in formulating parable-proverbs for young people to get by heart.

Only once in the Old Testament do we get a glimpse of schools that taught the alphabet, and there is a distinct suggestion that the teachers were not accorded the respect given to the Wise Men. At a time when Isaias was out of favour with the reigning king, probably Achaz, a party of drunks made a song about him. The passage, Isa. 28: 7–13, is more easily followed in the Knox version. The prophet, said the roysterers, was a nuisance, the way he kept saying the same things, just like an infant school teacher going over and over words that in Hebrew rhyme, *saw*, *qaw*, a command, a rule. Moreover he stammered, and his grammar was faulty—how could he expect anyone to take seriously his warnings of doom and disaster? The prophet's retort was more pointed than translation brings out, something like, 'Better heed the stammer or you'll get a foreign hammer.' That was not the kind of schooling the Wise Men went in for. In course of time their task was more and more to turn out competent and honest government officials.

ADMINISTRATION

This may seem a long way from Solomon's concern with plants and animals, yet it was in fact one of the twin roots from which the idea of Wisdom grew. Both were highly practical; Wisdom was never a speculative pursuit in Israel. The first root was skill in craftsmanship, as in Exod. 28: 3 and 31: 6. The second was administrative ability, as in Gen. 41: 39 and Deut. 34: 9. Both play their part in the story of Solomon, whose immense building work taxed not only his own 'wisdom' but that of his friend Hiram king of Tyre. Yet when God in a dream offered the young king his choice of a gift, Solomon's request for Wisdom was primarily for administrative skill, a bearing made clear in the story of the Judgment of Solomon (3 Kings 3). The same feeling for wisdom on its administrative side is the nerve of his prayer at the dedication of the Temple (3 Kings 8: 12 ff). In course of time, the craftsmanly side of wisdom more and more fell out of sight; the Wise Men concentrated on the arts of government.

In its complete form, exemplified by Ecclesiasticus, the Wisdom Movement came to be a system of education for boys of the leisured classes, to prepare them for what we should call public life. Indeed, Ecclesiasticus has been called 'a handbook for the civil service', though in fact its scope is considerably wider. A parallel might be found in the old Chinese education which was similarly designed to turn out a trustworthy official class. The examinations in Chinese literature largely concerned moral maxims, analects, not wholly unlike the parable-proverb of the Old Testament. But that old Chinese education lacked the strong religious emphasis of the Old Testament, that training in the Law of God which holds such a big place in the mind of Ben Sirach and the Wise Men generally.

THE STANDPOINT OF YOUTH

While the Wisdom Books abound in exhortations to paying humble attention to one's elders, they can at times firmly take the side of youth, as for instance in Wisd. 4: 7–14. The case of the young against the old is by no means overlooked. And the importance of happiness as an aid to growing up aright is generously recognised.

A striking example of a sudden statement of the case for the young is the Eliu episode in Job 32–7. This passage is generally regarded as a later addition, not by the main author of the book; its poetry is of an inferior type, and it can be left out without affecting the author's argument. Shortly before (chap. 30: 1) Job had complained of the attitude of young men. It looks as if a young man, full of ideas but not yet able to state them effectively, was stung into making an answer to the four old men who had for hours been running round in circles.

At first glance, it may seem strange that the young man shows no interest in the main originality of the book, the theory that suffering need not always be penal, it may be a test. On second thoughts, it looks more as if the young interpolator respects the central idea of the book: this new meaning of suffering is treated as a secret known only in Heaven, concealed from all on earth, even from Job himself. It is, however, possible that he was not interested. What annoyed him was that Job's elderly friends saw suffering only in terms of penalty, whereas it could also be a correction, a warning that one was on the wrong tack. This was a natural emphasis for one with his life still before him. Even more important, Eliu sees clearly the need for something in the way of inspiration or vision if there is to be a genuine serving of God. In general, he is an orthodox product of the Wise Men's system of education, accepting the ideas he had been taught—not the only instance we shall meet in which the young were less original than the old, even when their keenness of feeling led them to stress points of real consequence.[1] The worst of Eliu is that he does not know when to stop, so that he becomes as much of a bore as the old men he had interrupted.

THE ONLY ANSWER IS GOD

Neither the old nor the young give us the highlights in the Book of Job. Its most exciting speeches are those put in the mouth of God Himself (chaps. 38–41). They are exciting because they do not continue the argument, an argument which could never reach an end because the talkers were in the dark about the full character of the life after death. God's speeches break through this human clamour, not with an explanation—far from it!—but with a demand for submission. When all is said and done, the only answer to our questionings is: God Himself. It is more important to arrive at that (Job 42: 1–6) than to have an explanation which will fit tidily inside human heads, whether old or young. The wisdom of 'the heart' carries us deeper than any philosophy.

FOR READING

Besides passages mentioned in the chapter, try these:

1. *Education in General.* Prov. 2-7; Eccles. 10; Ecclus. 1–4.
2. *Public Life.* Eccles. 4: 13–16; 5: 7 to 7: 1; 8: 1–7. Wisdom 6–9; 14: 12–21 (which deals with the issue of king-worship). Ecclus—the whole book deals with it, but see especially chapter 32.

FOR DISCUSSION

Look at 2 Macc. 4: 7 ff. Does it altogether surprise you that, about a century after Ben Sirach, the gilded youth of Jerusalem flocked to the gymnasium opened for them shortly before the Macchabean revolt? Its intention was to draw them away from their ancestral religion and educate them in Hellenism. This Hellenisation was the policy of the king then reigning in Antioch-in-Syria, Antiochus IV, called Epiphanes, of whose dominions Palestine formed part. It is legitimate to feel that the education of the Wise Men was in some ways rather narrow in conception.

Part of our trouble comes from the fact that moralising has now

[1] See below, Chapter Four.

gone on for so long that we feel it as something stale and stuffy. It is so much an inheritance that it seems to have always existed. But to-day when the whole fabric of traditional life is challenged, can we find here any help in recapturing the first mood of delighted surprise? Can we recover something of the feeling in the Wisdom Books, that moralising is a new and exciting adventure? That it is more thrilling to be good than to be bad? The Wise Men never take the line that virtue is a soft option, the safe thing, achieved by following the crowd. They see it as a venture. Can we recover this spirit?

CHAPTER THREE

The Wisdom Movement: What it Did for Girls

THE WISE MEN did some very important work for girls but, Oriental fashion, they are reticent about it; the story has to be read between the lines and also in its results. What they did for girls was a by-product of their work for boys. For their boys' education had an unforeseen result: it upset the balance of the sexes, so that marriages were no longer happy.

Yet one of the traditional themes of the Wisdom Movement was the praise of happy marriage, along with counsels on how to get on with a wife. As still in the East, people married much younger than with us, sometimes at twelve or thirteen, rarely later than fifteen or sixteen. A phrase like 'the wife of thy youth', used by Malachias in his protest against divorce (Mal. 2: 13–15) had a vivid meaning. It is easy to see why the Wise Men had an eye on marriage as an extremely important item in the well-managed life they sought to open to their pupils.

The situation before them was very like the one created in our times in missionfield countries; the Western education provided for boys destroyed normal understanding between husband and wife. And modern missionaries hit on much the same solution as the Wise Men: they pushed on training for girls, whether by formal education or by training in home-making, and for the same reason: to restore the companionable element in marriage.

TRAINING FOR GIRLS

The course of events has to be pieced together. It is not altogether surprising that at first the Wise Men, bumping into the problem, were more aware of the bump than of the nature of the problem. The first to record the bump is the Ecclesiast.

At first sight Eccles. 9: 9 seems to be giving the conventional advice on marriage. But the context shows that he was advising the pursuit of pleasure as a means to forgetting his own disappointment in Wisdom. His more usual attitude seems to be that it is idle to hope for happiness through dealings with women (7: 27, 29). He is aware that something is amiss, but washes his hands of the problem.

Ben Sirach, the author of Ecclesiasticus, writing considerably later, probably about a century before the Macchabaean revolt, has more to say and takes a more hopeful view. True, he utters the traditional warnings about relations with women (9: 1–13; 25: 17–36), while in 42: 9–14 the anxieties a daughter can cause her father are feelingly described. But in 7: 25–7, sandwiched between two references to good wives (verses 21 and 28) he talks of the training of daughters as well as of sons. The advice given is on the severe side, but it is said to be the first time that anyone advocated, at least in writing, anything that could be called training for girls. (The remarkable training in the history and literature of her people received by Esther from her relative Mordechaeus seems to be an isolated instance which set up no sort of precedent.)

Quite possibly the Wise Men discussed the matter among themselves more freely than in books likely to get into the hands of their pupils, for there are grounds for thinking that definite steps were taken. One interpretation of the Valiant Woman passage with which Proverbs closes (Prov. 31: 10–31) is that it is a syllabus for the training of upper-class girls to make them fitter mates for the boys the Wise Men were handling in their schools. It is a curriculum for what we should call domestic science or home-making, but there is an odd little hint embedded in it. The passage is an acrostic on the Hebrew alphabet, a common type of memory aid. But it was of no use to the memories of those who did not know their letters. It looks as if girls could scramble into enough knowledge of reading to be helped by this device.

STATUS OF WOMEN

To-day, what strikes us in all these passages, favourable or unfavourable, is that women are considered solely in their effect upon men. Just here, Christianity has wrought one of its greatest revolutions, so great that we have difficulty nowadays in imagining what life would be like without it. But anyone who has had contact with the great non-Christian civilisations, in China, India or the Moslem East, has there found the punishment pronounced upon Eve in full force: 'Thou shall be under thy husband's power, and he shall have dominion over thee' (Gen. 3: 16).

Outside Christendom, woman rarely has status save as wife and mother. It was Christian virginity, beginning with the virgin marriage of Our Lady and St. Joseph, that started us back towards something that approximates more closely to the original relationship in Eden. As always, the New Eve played a part in reversing the harm done by the old Eve.

St. Paul sums up the new status of the Christian woman: her husband was her 'head' indeed, but she as much as he was important through her relation to her Creator, not to another creature.

Judaism was above most other cultures in the place it assigns to women—though it is only fair to mention the superiority of Egypt to other pagan lands. In the first chapter of the Bible it is firmly stated that woman as well as man is made to the image of God (Gen. 1: 27), and all through she was regarded as a responsible moral being, under obligation to keep the Law. Further, the Mosaic Law is quite remarkably fair to women, a fact driven home by our new knowledge of codes of comparable antiquity.

The Code of Hammurabi, a Babylonian king reigning a century or more after Abraham, and one of the very great men of history, lays down that in cases of assault, if the girl is a rich man's daughter the assaulter is to be put to death, but if she is a poor man's daughter, the girl herself is to die. The Mosaic

Law not only puts rich and poor on the same footing; it makes special provision to secure that the girl shall die only if she is certainly guilty, and provides a test by which to check her guilt (Deut. 22: 23–7).

Further, the only instance of an ordeal in the Mosaic Law is especially for the benefit of the woman whose husband suspects her of infidelity but has no proof. In general, Moses did a great service to his still barbarian people by insisting on the civilised practice of trial by evidence. In this one case, where evidence was lacking, he fell back on the primitive expedient of ordeal—a very mild ordeal, far less harmful than ducking witches or 'calling over the coals' (which means driving someone barefoot on to a bed of red hot coals). Incidentally, Moses is at pains to reassure the woman: if innocent, she cannot take harm (Num. 5: 12–37).

Had Susanna lived in Jerusalem, instead of in exile in Babylon, she could have demanded to clear herself by this ordeal. It took the quick wits of the young Daniel to devise evidence in the very case where the Law considered that it could not be got (Dan. 13).

THE JEWISH WOMAN'S HERITAGE

The Jewish woman thus had a heritage of far fairer treatment than her pagan neighbour. There were also unusual women in Jewish history. Esther and Judith, saviours of their people, are not regarded solely from the standpoint of their menfolk.

Yet in some ways the most unusual is the Sunamite who befriended Eliseus (4 Kings 4: 8 f.). She seems to be the first to blaze a new trail, so that in later times Jewish women were free to attach themselves to some notable rabbi and look after his needs—become in fact his 'ministering women', a freedom of enormous importance not only to Judaism but to Christianity.

There was thus in Judaism a sort of elasticity about the position of women which left the road open for further developments. But the actual development carried out by the Wise Men at first sight makes one rub one's eyes. Faced with this serious crisis in the way their new boys' education was working out, they coped in a charmingly unexpected way: they made a collection of folk-songs.

BETROTHAL SONGS

In the period before the Exile in Babylon, when the Chosen People in their two kingdoms of Israel and Juda could develop their customs in their own lands, a betrothal apparently took the form of songs sung to each other by the very young bride and bridegroom. Jeremias has several allusions to the custom (Jer. 7: 34; 16: 9; 33: 11). It has also been suggested that the prophet Osee, mourning over his own unfaithful wife, adapts one of these betrothal songs in his lament. That would have been a song from the district later called Galilee, for each region seems to have had its own traditional songs for these happy occasions.

After the Exile—this is one new theory—the Wise Men gathered these songs from different regions, strung them on a slender thread of story, and modernised the Hebrew so that it should be intelligible to their contemporaries. The language had changed a good deal during the Exile. Just as a Medieval carol needs a dress of modern English if we to-day are to enjoy it, so these betrothal songs needed a contemporary dress if people were to be at home with them.

But as with the carols, some touches of antiquity were allowed to remain as if to give a savour. For instance, the lovers in the story are very, very young, perhaps to excuse conduct which in later times would have been highly unconventional, especially for girls. No effort was made, however, to smooth out the different geographical backgrounds; hence at one moment the girl of the Canticle is singing to other Jerusalem girls, at the next frolicking through the spring lansdcape of Galilee (cf. Cant. 1: 4 and 2: 7; chap. 4). The Wise Men were not concerned to be realistic; there are other indications that in places they did not mean to be taken quite literally.

SPIRITUAL MEANING

Of course that is not the whole truth about the Canticle. It has indeed this practical purpose of giving a new ideal of human marriage at a period when marriages were too often coming to grief. But there was another theme, deriving from the ancient prophets. Osee seems to have been the first to develop the picture of Israel as the unfaithful wife of Yahweh, drawing from his own unhappy experience a new insight into the tenderness of God (Osee, chap. 2). Just as the prophet was prepared to take back the wayward Gomer, after a period of purification, so would God take back faithless Israel.

Yahweh—HE IS, the personal name of the God of Israel—would indeed require a period of purification (the Exile), but afterwards there would be a reconciliation and a re-marriage. This was fulfilled in the Return from Exile. One purpose of the betrothal songs was to celebrate this re-marriage of Yahweh with His wayward people.

Long after the practical crisis had faded from memory this second, mystical, purpose lived on, so that Jews saw in the Canticle primarily the love of Yahweh for Israel, Christians the love of Christ for His Church, or for the individual soul.

After ploughing through the moralisings of the Wise Men, it is refreshing to leave them coping with their most troublesome problem by setting boys and girls to sing love songs to each other.

FOR READING

Besides looking up the references given in the chapter, read the Canticle of Canticles, or as much of it as you feel inclined for. Scholars are not yet fully agreed as to where the various songs begin and end. Mgr. Knox gives one set of divisions, taking the allusions to Solomon as historic fact; and that is one profitable way of taking the book.

But another approach is possible; we may regard the allusions to Solomon as a sort of game between the young lovers. To the girl, her boy was as good as Solomon; they made an arbour to represent a royal chamber and pretended that water from the well was wine. In this way of looking at it, the best division is into seven songs:

1. Cant. 1: 1–2: 7. The girl sings first, telling how her brothers set her to work guarding the vineyards, so that she became very sunburnt. But for all her brave front to the Jerusalem girls ('black but beautiful'), her lover has the sense to realise that she needs reassurance about her complexion (verses 7 and 9, etc.).

Palestine vines are not propped but are left to trail on the ground, an easy prey to two- and four-legged marauders. Jackals (foxes) are specially partial to grapes. Hence the watch-tower, often a square of rough stones, which can be roofed with branches as vintage approaches; in July the whole family usually camps out in its vineyard. Quite likely the watch-tower served for the 'cellar of wine' of 2: 4.

In 1: 7–10 the boy answers the girl's first song, in 11–13 the girl goes on with their game. From 1:14 to 2: 7 they sing turn about, the girl's songs being rather the longer. Among the thorn scrub, about the height of heather, they find narcissi (lilies among thorns) which scent the air. The last verse (2: 7) is a refrain to be met again later, marking the end of a poem.

2. Cant. 2: 8–3: 5. The boy comes to help her chase away the jackals. After this happy day they come home together, but the girl cannot sleep. Some think it was rather a dream or a fantasy that she ran out to look for her boy (3: 1–5). They are very young; their love is still largely play.

3. Cant. 3: 6–5: 1. The whole of this song is the boy's.

4. Cant. 5: 2–6: 2. The boy comes to see her, but for once the girl plays the coquette and has to pay for it.

5. Cant. 6: 3–8: 4. The episode of the Sulamite (6: 12–7: 9) is a puzzle and does not seem to fit into any interpretation of the story. Perhaps the boy went off after a professional dancer, but returned to his own girl in the end.

6. Cant. 8: 5–7. In this tiny song, the words used of Solomon's bride (3: 6) are repeated to mark the contrast: the village girl is not carried in a litter but walks leaning on her lover's arm.

7. Cant. 8: 8–15. The match is made up. The girl stands silent, bursting with pride, while her lover refuses to bargain. The brothers demand a fantastic bride-price, but instead of trying to beat them down he offers them yet more—in Oriental eyes the most touching evidence of his love. After all—to revert to the mystical meaning—neither Yahweh's love for Israel nor Christ's for the Church was entirely without cost.

FOR DISCUSSION

Those who want a practical problem can find one in any aspect of the 'boy meets girl' question.

Yet another point is in some ways more practical, though to some disconcerting. This religious view of marriage is a speciality of Judaism, then of Christianity, above all the idea that human marriage reflects the relationship of God with His Chosen Community, whether Israel or the Church. This is an image which many people find troubling, but our religion is quite clear about its validity.

Further, the relation of God to a single human soul may be viewed as a marriage: nuns, for instance, are the spouses of God. When young girls in the early Church sought to give themselves wholly to God, they seem to have devised this language themselves.

We meet it in St. Agnes for instance, the twelve-year-old who explained to her judge that she could not accept any of the young men who wanted to marry her because she was already betrothed. Like the other virgin martyrs, she was rich as well as pretty; the law wanted to be sure that such a large dowry was in the care of some responsible male. It was here that the question of women's status found its crux: could even a very rich girl belong wholly to God? Against the legal assumption, Agnes and other girls—such young girls!—opposed the idea of their betrothal to Our Lord Himself, and preferred death to taking a husband. It seems to have been entirely spontaneous language on their part.

NOTE

A question likely to form in our minds is: Did the Wise Men achieve anything of value in the training of girls? The answer is to be found in the New Testament. Our Lord removed the last great disability under which Jewish women laboured—divorce. The result was an extraordinary outburst of energy, especially in the direction of 'ministering', i.e. the highly developed charitable work of the first Christians.

All the same, the New Testament covers a crisis—the Jewess was far ahead of her pagan neighbours. We glean this partly from St. Luke, the one non-Jew among the New Testament writers, who as a doctor had access to homes more freely than other men. Clearly, what he met in pagan homes did not prepare him for the women he met in Jewish homes. His observant eyes are our chief witness to what women were good for in Jewish circles in the time of the Apostles.

Further, St. Paul seems to have run into difficulties through assuming that all women were equal to the Jewesses he had known in boyhood and youth. What may have misled him was that the pagan women of his native city, Tarsus, were renowned in the Roman world for their modesty of dress and demeanour. When he had to deal with women converts from paganism, he found that they could not give what he had asked from Jewesses. This was notably the case in Corinth, the most corrupt city of the Roman world. It is there that we first find St. Paul speaking of the life of virginity for girls, and obtaining a response. Later, however, he seems to have realised that it was wiser to go slow. He never went back on his principles, but he did practice them more cautiously. In his later epistles he seems to feel that most women were better married. But he never took the line that certain aspects of Christian practice were closed to them.

As an illustration: among the Jews, as said above, women were at liberty to care for a religious teacher; they were also at liberty to go out on errands of charity. It was not so with pagan women. Most sensible people would have advised St. Paul to tell all his women converts of pagan origin to stay at home. Instead, he merely advised a rigid modesty of dress and demeanour—most necessary protection in the streets of a pagan town—and used plain language about gadding and gossip. But it was the Jewesses who gave him a starting-point. The training devised by the Wise Men had made the Jewess a person in her own right, and opened to her a wider field of activity than pagan women enjoyed. On this foundation Our Lord could build. St. Paul, following Him up, saw that the Christian woman of pagan background needed time to catch up with the Jewess, but was perfectly capable of such development if she was not unduly pushed. . . . Similar problems have arisen in mission-field countries in our own times.

CHAPTER FOUR

Ezechiel and the Angry Young Men

EZECHIEL, a younger contemporary of Jeremias, was called to the prophetic office after his deportation to Babylon (Ezech. 2 and 3: 1–11, where 'son of man' means simply 'human being'). During the first ten or eleven years of his ministry Jeremias was alive—sometimes only just alive—in Jerusalem. Both prophets lived through the last days of the Jewish monarchy, culminating in the siege and destruction of Jerusalem by Nabuchodonosor in 586 B.C.

THE DEPORTEES

Ezechiel was one of the second batch of deportees to Babylon. The First Deportation, a small affair, had included Daniel, and was little more than a levy of likely boys for the service of the king in Babylon. The object had been to drive home to Joachim (Joakim), king of Juda, that he was not an independent monarch merely because Assyria had fallen; he was a vassal of the new power, Babylon. The Second Deportation was more serious. It was the response to Joachim's foolish revolt, during the years when Nabuchodonosor was busy securing himself on the throne after his accession. Joachim died before Nabuchodonosor could act, leaving his young son, Joachin or Jechonias, to face the storm.

It broke in 598 B.C. when Jechonias had reigned only three months. Jechonias himself was deported, as was the high priest, a number of leaders and of young men who might have grown into leaders, as well as the craftsmen who in time of war would have turned into armourers (Jer. 29: 2). Ezechiel, a priest, was probably included because the Babylonians felt it best to have such a forceful character under their own eye. Actually, like

Jeremias, Ezechiel was entirely loyal to Babylon once the new king of Juda had sworn a special oath of loyalty; king Sedecias had to journey to Babylon to take this oath with due ceremony.

It was the younger members of this Second Deportation who formed the group we are thinking of as Angry Young Men. Ezechiel's mission to them thus fell between the Second Deportation and the Third, the one we think of as *the* Exile *par excellence.*

During those eleven years, the important background events took place in Jerusalem. The Babylonian end is little more than that the Jews were assigned their own settlements and, like other deportees, allowed to follow their own customs under the rule of their own elders. Any hint of rebellion was severely dealt with (Jer. 29: 21–23), but otherwise they were humanely treated.

IN JERUSALEM: SEDECIAS AND JEREMIAS

In Jerusalem, however, the pivotal factor was the weak character of King Sedecias. Nabuchodonosor may have selected him as his puppet-king with the idea that he would never have the strength of mind to head a rebellion. If so, he judged amiss. Sedecias became the tool of stronger minds, and not only the political leaders of the Jews. Within a few years, Egypt was at her traditional game of inciting the small states of Western Asia to revolt.

The leaders in Jerusalem had no business to be taken in; almost exactly the same had happened a century and a half earlier, when the personalities were Sennacherib of Assyria, King Ezechias of Juda, and the prophet Isaias. The phrase we still use, 'a broken reed,' was coined by Isaias to describe the traditional Egyptian policy of getting others to pull her chestnuts out of the fire for her (Isa. 36: 6).

Under Sedecias, Jeremias continued his predecessor's policy of trying to keep his country free from these dangerous entanglements. But Sedecias let himself be jockeyed into rebellion, incidentally breaking his oath of allegiance. Hence the severity of Nabuchodonosor's treatment. After he had taken and destroyed Jerusalem in 586 B.C., he had Sedecias blinded and sent in chains to Babylon. He then deported practically the whole population, save the peasantry and a 'skeleton staff' of men of position left to run the country (Jer. 39).

All this was happening during the years when Ezechiel faced the Angry Young Men. The Second Deportation had reached Babylon in a bad frame of mind. In spite of this, Jeremias had seen that all hope for the future lay with them, not with the weak king and his headstrong advisers in Jerusalem. But his intervention in this sense (Jer. 29) produced only a letter from the high priest in exile to his deputy in Jerusalem, advising him to put the prophet in the stocks. Clearly much had to be done before the deportees would fulfil Jeremias's expectation. That they ultimately did so is due to Ezechiel, who for ten long years hammered away at them to get them to see sense.

WRONG IDEAS OF GOD

The root of their wrong attitude was utterly unworthy ideas of God. For two hundred years prophet after prophet had tried to bring Israel and Juda back to the true idea of God learned from Moses, but with little success. The Chosen People had demoted Yahweh—HE IS—from the status of the One True God to that of a common or garden national god, whose job it was to be on the side of his people no matter how they behaved. . . . It is instructive to reflect that to-day the gods of that type are historical curiosities; they disappeared with their peoples. Only the God of Israel is still active—because He was, and is, a very different kind of deity.

The situation had not developed all at once. For generations, friction between the prophets and the powerful classes had been increasing. There was a widespread feeling that Yahweh was forgetting His place, making demands which no other god made, which no god had a right to make. Who had ever heard of a god who minded the oppression of the poor by the rich, or a little judicious sacrificing to other deities? If a god got his dues in cultus, he had no business to bother them about their morals. If Yahweh did not mend His manners they would pay Him out by transferring their allegiance elsewhere. Far from giving up idolatry in Babylon, the deportees at first showed signs of yet further experimenting. The whole future of monotheism was at stake.

Against this, Ezechiel urged a fundamental fact: Yahweh was the only God who had *chosen* His people; chosen them on terms to which they had themselves subscribed, making themselves a party to the Covenant which He had made with them on Sinai. All other national gods had come into existence along with their peoples, a projection of their hopes, fears and ambitions, a personification of the natural forces on which they depended for the means of existence. Yahweh had never been that kind of god. He had done Israel the extraordinary honour of choosing them from among all the peoples of the earth; they had responded by insulting Him, degrading Him in their minds to the level of the gods of the surrounding peoples.

And yet, such a queer mixture are human beings, there was a sort of backwash of feeling that after all Yahweh was *their* God. They would willingly stick to Him if only He would fall in with their ideas of how a god should behave. All He had to do was to copy His own behaviour of over a hundred years earlier, when He had turned back the Assyrian king Sennacherib from before Jerusalem. That astounding deliverance had in fact given rise to a superstition: Yahweh would *never* allow His city to be destroyed, His temple profaned; that was something on which they could safely gamble.

True, even at the time the prophet Michaeas had protested, and here to-day was that other fool Jeremias doing the same—but that was the sort of nonsense one had learned to expect from prophets (Mich. 3: 11; Jer. 7[1]; and see Jer. 26, which connects the two prophets). Superstition had in fact allied itself

[1] Silo was the national sanctuary before David captured Jerusalem (v. 12). Ephraim was the chief of the Ten Tribes of the Northern Kingdom of Israel (v. 15), destroyed by the Assyrians over a century before Jeremias.

with wishful thinking. It was only when wishfulness came crashing to earth with the walls and buildings of Jerusalem, including the Temple, that the Angry Young Men became ready to listen to Ezechiel; he had been right when all around were wrong. But they already knew what line he wanted them to take.

WHERE THEY WERE RIGHT

So far, the deportees were quite simply in the wrong. Now comes a point where they deserve sympathy. There they were, young, uprooted, torn from their homeland and all decent prospects, and why? Simply because the older generation had betrayed them. The old had done the wrong and the young had to foot the bill. This situation they expressed in a proverb which Jeremias met in Jerusalem as well as Ezechiel in Babylon: 'The fathers have eaten sour grapes and the children's teeth are set on edge' (Jer. 31: 29; Ezech. 18: 2).

Here, they deserve some respect, if only for getting hold, imperfectly and clumsily, of a new insight. In ancient theory, the unit of moral responsibility was the community, not the individual. It was to the community that God, through Moses, had promised prosperity if they kept the Law, disaster if they disobeyed it. In the many disasters which disobedience had brought on them nobody felt that innocent individuals had anything to resent; they were part and parcel of the community.

But towards the end of the monarchy, oppression developed within the Chosen People. It was no longer a case of disobedient Israel and Juda suffering at the hands of Philistines, Edomites, Aramaeans, Assyrians and so forth, but of good, poor Israelites suffering at the hands of bad, rich ones. That was what first awakened criticism of the ancient theory.

Actually, the Angry Young Men were not in the forefront of this movement of thought; they merely got as far as opposing one generation to another. Just as the young Eliu did not go really deep in his criticism of Job and the old men, so these Young Men barely touched the fringes of the problem of innocent suffering, and very nearly wrecked any possibility of a solution by bad temper. They were right in seeing that the old theory did not wholly fit their case; but they were in danger of spoiling a real insight by a snarling, self-justifying mood which would lead nowhere. Ezechiel's greatness was in finding the beginnings of a road which ultimately led somewhere.

In coping with this mood, Ezechiel had his hands tied. No one yet knew anything of rewards and punishments after death; they still had the outlook described briefly in our second chapter (see p. 14). Ezechiel thus had to make out his case solely in terms of this life. And it has to be admitted that the case sounds oddly in ears accustomed to the full Christian revelation. He had to prove to the Angry Young Men that they personally deserved what had happened to them—if only by sharing their elders' wrong ideas about God. He was the first in Israel, perhaps the first in human history, to teach the doctrine of individual responsibility. That was his special greatness.

What we have in Ezechiel is the very first teaching of individual responsibility, though Jeremias was feeling his way to something similar. Naturally the line he takes is to us in some ways 'in the air', unrelated both to full teaching on the life after death, and to an all-round doctrine of suffering, its place in the life of community and individual, its varied values. Ezechiel does not get as far as the Book of Job, with its suggestion that suffering may be a test; he is still limited to the ideas of penalty and correction. Like the author of Job, he deserves the credit due to someone who has the first glimpse of something new, something which he still does not see 'in the round', but which has immense possibilities. Inadequate as his treatment must sound in Christian ears, it was he above all who prevented the deportees from losing themselves in a cul-de-sac. The immediate necessity was not to answer all possible questions—we cannot do that even now—but to hold open a road for the future.

Once Jerusalem had fallen, sweeping away in its fall both the superstition and the wishfulness which had stood in his way, Ezechiel's painful ministry bore fruit. A considerable body of the deportees conformed spontaneously to the attitude he had long urged on them. The new outlook is preserved in the *De*

Profundis, a psalm from the heart of Israel's purgation which the genius of the Church has applied to purgatory. There is a more diffuse account of the same temper and attitude in Baruch, chapters 1, 2 and 3: 1–8, where the rallying point is the exiled king Jechonias. And his name points at once to the fruit of Ezechiel's ministry. It was through Jechonias, and his grandson Zorobabel, that Our Lord could claim descent from David (Matt. 1: 12, 13). The road which Ezechiel opened was indeed a through road.

TWO QUESTIONS, NOT ONE

When we are faced by great and inexplicable suffering, there are two questions clamouring for an answer, not one: Why do we suffer? and, How should we suffer? In itself, suffering only too easily crushes, twists, frustrates; it is an instrument of death. To make it an instrument of life, the How is more urgent than the Why, for unless the How is found and practised, people will not have the mental balance to find a worthwhile answer to the Why. The greatest spirits of our race have all had a glimpse of this. To the Why, Buddha, Confucius, the Persian Dualists, the Stoics, Mohammed have returned very varied answers. But they agree surprisingly on the How, and here they are very close to Ezechiel.[1] Suffering destroys those who are simply defiant, because under the defiance is an erroneous demand, the notion that reality owes us something. Abandon that claim. Be just. Be humble. Accept reality as something to which we owe all but which owes us nothing. In a word, be filial. So we shall find not so much an answer as a way, a road wherein the How becomes a source of strength and enrichment. Even men who did not know the One True God have seen thus far. Part of our difficulty with Ezechiel is that, though he knew the One True God he did not know the full depth of His generosity. Not all had faith enough to respond to what we, enjoying our rich banquet, are tempted to dismiss as meagre fare.

[1] Kipling's poem on the king sold into slavery seizes the point:
Not with an outcry to Allah, nor any complaining
He answered his name at the muster and stood to the chaining.

FOR READING

1. *Individual Responsibility.* The lesson was first taught to the prophet himself, in Ezech. 3: 15–21. The key passage is chapter 18.

2. *The Siege of Jerusalem,* chaps. 4, 5, 6, 7.

3. *Sedecias.* Ezech. 12: 1–16, cf. 4 Kings 25: 1–7. Ezech. 17: 1–21, where a Messianic passage (verses 22–4) follows immediately—after Sedecias there was no King of the line of David until the Messias Himself. The first eagle (verse 3) is Nabuchodonosor, who deposed Jechonias and replaced him by Sedecias. The second eagle is the pharoah who incited Sedecias to revolt, and to his breach of oath (verses 11–21). This breach of oath clearly horrified Ezechiel, who returns to it again in 21: 25–6.

4. *Elegy on the Last Kings of Juda,* chap. 19. It omits the one who died in his homeland, Joachim; the other three all died in exile. The Lioness of Juda had reared two cubs, two kings who were the choice of the people themselves. The first, Joachaz, was carried off to Egypt by the Pharoah Nechao whom Nabuchodonosor soon after defeated in 605 B.C., the year of the first, small, deportation. The second, Jechonias, was at this very time an exile in Babylon. The third, the choice not of the people but of Nabuchodonosor, was now on his way to Babylon blinded and in bonds; he is the one most in mind (verses 2, 10–14). The Elegy stresses that he had brought his fate on himself; the fire which destroyed him was of his own kindling.

NOTE

To Ezechiel, Sedecias is little more than a symbol, the utterly unworthy descendant of David. By contrast, Jeremias shows us the human being, weak, unable to hold his own, but amiable and often wishing to do better than he dared. At times he dared a good deal. Though he handed Jeremias over to his enemies, he came to the rescue on learning that they had thrown him into a cistern. And it was Sedecias who personally secured to the imprisoned prophet his ration during the siege (Jer. 37: 10 to the end of 38). For all his sternness in encounter, Jeremias seems to have had a soft spot for the ill-fated king. When it was no longer his duty to be severe, he mourns over him quite simply as the last of the House of David (Lam. 4: 20, where 'Christ' means 'anointed king', i.e. Sedecias). As so often, the Old Testament lets us see people and events from more than one angle, and builds up a likeness in the round.

OPTIONAL

If you are interested, try also the following:

5. *Ezechiel's Wife.* The present writer has to own that at times Ezechiel irritates her intensely, and she forgives him chiefly because his wife loved him—no small tribute considering what a maddening person he must have been to have about the house. Look again at chapter 4, where he is told to live on the same rations as the besieged in Jerusalem. Lying on the left side or the right (verses 4 ff.) alludes to the fact that in ancient times the points of the compass were reckoned from the east, not the north; so that right is south (the kingdom of Juda) and left is north (the kingdom of Israel). His wife must have had a tough time with him by night as well as by day, when she had to cope with his peculiar and inconvenient feeding arrangements. All through his years of struggle with the Angry Young Men, there was someone who loved him and believed in him, believed, too, that God spoke through him, accommodating herself silently to the odd conduct that Divine command laid upon him. When she died, Ezechiel was forbidden to mourn for her, as a sign that the Exiles were not to mourn the fall of Jerusalem; a passage (chap. 24: 15–27) poignant through its restraint.

6. *Some Famous Passages.* (a) Chap. 15, a new use of the Vine metaphor. Israel had long been thought of as Yahweh's vineyard (e.g. Isa. 5: 1–7), a theme taken up again by Our Lord in the parable of the Wicked Husbandmen (Matt. 21: 33–44). In Ezech. 15: 4, the two ends are the Northern Kingdom of Israel, destroyed by the Assyrians in 721 B.C., and the Southern Kingdom of Juda, destroyed by Nabuchodonosor in 586 B.C. (b) Chap. 21. Verses 8–17 are known as The Song of the Sword of Yahweh. Verses 18–23 give a lively picture of Nabuchodonosor consulting the augurs to decide which route his army should take, whether down the east side of the Jordan and round the south of the Dead Sea to take Jerusalem in the rear, or by the more usual route via Galilee, the passes of Carmel and the Coastal Plain. (c) Chap. 27, the second of three oracles against Tyre which Nabuchodonosor was then besieging. The city on its island, half a mile from the shore, is likened to a ship. (d) Chap. 32: 17 ff., Sheol, the underworld of the dead to which all these kings and conquerors would come. Assur (verse 22) is Assyria. The only penalty for these oppressors which Ezechiel foresees is that they would be levelled down to their victims—in Sheol all were on an equality, and

of course it was the great of this world who would mind it most. It is well to remind ourselves that this is ALL that Ezechiel knew about the life after death—i.e. he knew that souls survive, and that death is a leveller. In the seventeenth century the Catholic poet James Shirley (1596–1666) wrote a play with a pagan setting. In the songs composed for it he stresses especially this sense of death the leveller; the best known is the one beginning 'The glories of our blood and state', which can be found in Palgrave's *Golden Treasury*.

FOR DISCUSSION

In considering the Angry Young Men of our own time, is there any help in the fact that Ezechiel had to handle his own similar problem without appeal to rewards and punishments after death? To-day, of course, such Young Men would not threaten to choose other gods, they would call themselves atheists or agnostics. But at bottom the reason would be the same: the True God has refused to be a tame pocket god acting in the way they consider suitable. Here are some thoughts.

1. Any attempt to-day to appeal to the life after death is apt to be countered by 'There's pie in the sky when you die.' What has fallen out of men's mental picture is purgatory. The whole idea of purgation needs to be reawakened before it is possible to get across much about Heaven and Hell. To some extent such a re-awakening is taking place spontaneously. The widespread interest in reincarnation means chiefly that in some minds at least the idea of a *temporary* punishment after death is coming to life again. (The word 'temporary' is more generally understood than 'temporal'.) As far as it goes, this has a good side. Purgatory, far more than Heaven or Hell, is a natural human insight, and its loss has done immense harm to the quality of religion and irreligion.

2. In any mention of Heaven it is well to remember that some Protestants and practically all ex-Protestants have come to equate it with a state of perfected natural happiness, in other words, with what we should call Limbo. A good sample is John Buchan's poem 'Fisher Jamie' (No. 152 in *The Northern Muse*) where the dead poacher cannot be happy unless he gets some poaching in Heaven. In such discussions it is well to avoid the word *supernatural*, which to non-Catholics suggests a mixture of the miraculous and the occult. Where words bear different meanings to different speakers, it is best to use neutral terms even if they are long-winded, 'temporary

punishment', 'the same kind of happiness as we enjoy on earth, only carried to perfection', and so on.

3. Behind the bad temper there is real spiritual bewilderment and a sense of betrayal. But there is a misinterpretation, a tendency to think that they have been betrayed by the generation before (just like Ezechiel's Angry Young Men). That generation in turn feels itself betrayed by those who lived before 1914. Clearly this is a barren road, ending in bogs. If people are to be helped find a road that gets anywhere, they will have to be persuaded, tactfully, to face some disagreeable facts. For instance, the real betrayal has come from those who have innoculated so many with the idea that life owes us all a good time. This is the only ideal they know, and it has turned to ashes in their mouth. A few years ago Communism offered an ideal; to-day, it has partly lost its appeal to those with any streak of idealism. It is among these frustrated idealists that we meet our Angry Young People. Their trouble, as with their prototypes in the Old Testament, is a false claim, the idea that reality owes them all they want. It owes us nothing, a terribly hard truth to lay to heart, yet the only genuine liberation.

4. Part of the difficulty of making any direct reference to Christianity is that people have lost not its doctrines but the foundations underlying those doctrines. This is where the Old Testament may be of enormous help to us. Our Lord could take for granted ideas and attitudes which to-day have melted out of men's minds. Perhaps the greatest difficulty of any apostolate lies just here.

CHAPTER FIVE

What Do We Mean by Prophets?

OUR READINGS in Ezechiel may have left a question: Why had he so little to say about the future? Surely a prophet is one who utters predictions? That is so to-day, but it was not so in Old Testament times. Both the Hebrew word *nebi'* and its Greek equivalent *propheta* mean a spokesman, one who speaks for another. Indeed, in the Hebrew Bible, God says to Moses, 'Thy brother [Aaron] shall be thy *nebi'*—thy prophet, the one to do the actual talking to the people (Exod. 7: 1).

SPOKESMEN

While the word could thus be used of one human being in relation to another, a prophet was more usually the spokesman of a god. Prophecy in this sense was an institution of all the Semitic peoples. Nearly every god had his prophets, men of special psychic gifts, second sight and so forth, cultivated by training, to enable them to go into ecstasy and answer the questions put to their gods. These questions were usually entirely practical: If we go to war shall we win? Shall I have a son to succeed me? Where shall I find such and such a lost article? In the earlier parts of the Old Testament we shall find prophets of the True God who did not disdain to deal with such matters. (See for instance 1 Kings 1; 8 and 9; 10: 1–16; 4 Kings 3: 4ff.) Evidently, then, we have here one further instance of the way the Chosen People started much where other peoples did, then went somewhere quite different.

The point where the road forked was first and foremost the character of Yahweh. Even among the heathen, the character of the god served did much to decide what sort of men his prophets were. Balaam, the pagan seer called in to curse the

Israelites advancing on Palestine, must have served a fairly respectable god, hence his susceptibility to the presence of the True God. The reward for his integrity was that he uttered a Messianic prophecy (Num. 22, 23 and 24). But the prophets who served the foul Melkart, the baal or lord of Tyre, were a very different breed (3 Kings 18).

Clearly, prophesying so conceived was not only prediction; it could deal with past or present as much as with the future. And this brings us to an important point. Other gods were apt to be manifestations of the forces of nature; Yahweh was the Author and Lord of nature. Here again the road forked. Gods who represented natural forces could not take a firm line about anything that finds an actual place in nature; they were in a weak position when it came to what men ought to do as distinct from what they often do do. Just because Yahweh was nature's Lord, He was also the Source and Maintainer of the moral order, the thing that says 'ought' or 'ought not' even in the face of what is actually happening.

A prophet of Yahweh thus stood in an exceptional relationship to morality. A great deal of his work consisted in protesting —speaking for God—when morality was outraged. And since the moral framework of our lives is also a social and political framework, the community's standards to a considerable extent conditioning the individual's chances of doing right, the prophets of Yahweh were much concerned with social and political issues. To denounce wrongdoing, on the part of individual or community, in the past or the present, was prophesying quite as much as foretelling the outcome of such wrongdoing in the future.

And this close association with morality led to something further: prophecy about the future was always conditional. Right up to the last minute, with disaster ready to break like a wave on their heads, people could save themselves by repentance and a genuine reformation of conduct. Because God is good, He is bound to punish evil-doing. Because He is good, He will never go back on His covenant and utterly cast away His people.

The Hebrew conception of history was thus profoundly prophetic. A whole section of the Hebrew Bible, from Josue to the end of Kings, is classed as 'the former prophets', not because these books enshrine many stories about prophets, though they do, but because they enshrine the Divine estimate of the deeds recorded. This is the principle governing the selection of events. The Divine estimate is not always put into words. A Hebrew historian must not be taken to approve all he relates. Even though there is at times direct moral comment, more often disapproval is indirectly expressed through the outcome of the situation.

PROPHECY ABOUT THE FUTURE

Prophecy about the present dealt mainly with Israel's sins. But since the present is the immeasurably small moment in which the future becomes the past, prophecy about the present slides almost unnoticed into prophecy about the future, at first the fairly immediate future. The prophet Nathan's handling of the David and Bethsabee incident is good a sample (2 Kings 11 and 12: 1–25.

But as widespread national apostasy developed towards the end of the Monarchy period, the prophets began to foretell disaster on a much greater scale, disaster involving the whole unrepentant nation. The prophets of Israel were the only men in Western Asia to 'discern the signs of the times'. They saw what the rise of the new power, Assyria, in the ninth–eighth century, was going to mean to that small world of small nations; they first foresaw the policy of deportation initiated by the Assyrians and developed by the Chaldaeans (the correct name for those we call the Babylonians). This deportation, said Amos, Osee, Michaeas, Isaias and many others, would be God's instrument for the punishment of His faithless people. But since God could never be faithless, they saw beyond the punishment to something lying further off, the restoration through return from Exile.

And here we come to something most remarkable: out of this insight into restoration from Exile a large proportion of Messianic prophecy grew. Beyond the Return, God's spokesmen dimly discerned something else, something that had kinship with the Return yet outclassed it, something that would illustrate the same principles in a more drastic, final way. Hence quite a few prophecies of Return fade into, or are intermingled with, prophecies either of the Messianic Age or of the Messias in person. (For example, see Mich. 4 and 5.) Not all the points belong to both planes of distance; it is not always easy to sort them out. But the meeting-ground is always the nature of God Himself.

If the short-term predictions of the Hebrew prophets may have some meagre parallels elsewhere, their long-term predictions are unique—so unique that they have altered our whole conception of prophecy, equating it more and more with prediction. This is a legitimate development of language. But if we are to understand the Old Testament we have to go behind the development and learn to think of prophecy as spokesmanship, the making known of God's mind, about past or present as much as about the future, by men specially called to that task.[1]

PROFESSIONAL PROPHETS

And now another question may be forming in our minds: Since the Israelites knew that a prophet was a spokesman of God, why did they not instantly believe him? Part of the answer lies in the fact, mentioned earlier, that prophecy was an institution. We hear several times of 'schools of the prophets' where 'sons of the prophets'—young men of suitable gifts—were trained for their task. This is one reason why a prophet, often nameless, appears so often in the story. Up to a point, these schools of the prophets did good work. But inevitably they meant that prophecy became professionalised, open to the dangers of professionalism.

The chief temptation rose out of the fact that where prophets were held in honour, they might be supported at public expense, or at any rate get a fee from their hearers. There was thus a strong temptation to say what the man who paid them wanted

[1] In the New Testament too prophecy is not always prediction. More often it seems to be a kind of ecstatic utterance of the truths of God.

to hear, particularly if he was the king. As the sky darkened with the rise, first of Assyria, then of the Chaldaean dynasty in Babylon, men wanted above all to be reassured. The prophet who would tell them they had nothing to fear was eagerly listened to (Isa. 30: 10—better in the Knox).

The result was an increasing tension between true and false prophets, and an increasing stress on the element of vocation in making a prophet, rather than of training (e.g. Amos 7: 10 ff.). The prophet's call came to be felt as a strong constraint; against his will, the true prophet found himself under an overmastering inner compulsion to tell the people the unwelcome truths they had no wish to hear (Amos 3: 8; Jer. 1: 4–10).

DISCERNMENT

Those who rejected the true prophets had a measure of excuse. The tests laid down in the Law of Moses were not entirely helpful. The first (Deut. 13: 1–5) insists that no true prophet would attempt to beguile Israel into the worship of foreign gods. The second (Deut. 18: 20–2) adds that a true prophet would be known because his prophecies would be fulfilled—which gave little help before the event. When four hundred prophets, speaking for Yahweh and so fulfilling the first test, assured Achab that he would take the city of Ramoth Galaad, why believe the solitary prophet who said he would meet his death there? (3 Kings 22, with a glance back to chapters 18 and 21.) And in later times, why believe Jeremias in preference to prophets who assured the king, his advisers and the populace that the Chaldaeans (Babylonians) would never take Jerusalem? (Jer. 5: 26–31; 14: 11–16; 23: 16–40.)

The answer is that God always leaves room for moral and spiritual discernment. Up to the time of the Exile the true prophets grew more and more unpopular. Yet they had their following, men with the moral and spiritual insight which enabled them to recognise the voice of God when they heard it. It is largely to these supporters of the true prophets that we owe the very existence of the Old Testament. It was they who secretly passed round copies of the prophets' oracles, preserved them, copied them, gathered them into books and handed them on to us. What needs to be laid to heart is that such an act of recognition was perfectly possible, to men of genuine integrity. Where integrity had been lost, God did not offer the mathematical certainty which the crooked-minded are apt to demand. Only to the morally prepared could it be evident that this or that message came indeed from God.

FOR READING

Besides looking up the passages alluded to in the text, try these:

1. *Schools of the Prophets.* In 1 Kings 19: 18 ff., 'the naioth' or 'dwellings' seem to have housed men in training as prophets under the aegis of Samuel. Later, such 'schools' are mentioned only in the records of the Northern Kingdom of Israel (the Ten Tribes that broke away from the Dynasty of David in the days of Solomon's son Roboam). Eliseus had a good deal to do with such centres, both of training and of communal life for trained prophets. There were such centres at Bethel (4 Kings 2: 3), Jericho (2: 5), and by the Jordan (6: 1). For stories, see 4 Kings 2; verses 23–4 suggest that such prophets were marked with some sort of tonsure. Since Bethel was one of the places where Yahweh—yes, Yahweh!—was worshipped under the image of a calf (3 Kings 12: 25–33) its inhabitants had a powerful 'economic motive' for hating true prophets; the children took their cue from their parents.

2. *False Prophets*, i.e. those who yielded to the temptation of saying what those who paid them wanted to hear. Osee 9: 7–8; Mich. 3, esp. verses 5 and 11.

3. *The Widening Rift Between True Prophets and the Authorities.* Amos 7: 10–17. Amasias was the priest of the calf-shrine of Yahweh at Bethel. Jer. 26, with its interesting reference to Michaeas—the author of the book, not the Michaeas who got into trouble with Achab a hundred years earlier. We should not otherwise know that the later Michaeas had also been in trouble with the authorities. 4 Kings 21: 1–18, esp. verses 10 and 16; after the death of Ezechias, the Book of Kings never again mentions a prophet by name, not even Jeremias; it was too dangerous. By Jewish tradition, one of those who perished under Manasses was Isaias, sawn in two with a wooden saw; this is

probably referred to in Heb. 11: 37. The climax comes with Jeremias (Jer. 28, 29).

After the return from Exile the rift closed. Prophets were once more held in honour. There were fewer of them, and there seem to have been no false prophets. In the end prophecy died out, until it was revived by the Jordan in the person of John the Baptist. It is also worth reflecting that, among other things, Our Lord was the last and greatest of the Hebrew prophets.

FOR DISCUSSION

Let us take the climax of the long conflict between the prophets and the authorities, the case of Jeremias. He was accused of what we should call 'spreading alarm and despondency', hampering his country's war effort in her hour of desperate peril during the siege by Nabuchodonosor. (Jer. 38: 4—read the whole chapter and the preceding one.) The question raised is: Just how far do the claims of patriotism go?

There are two main conceptions of patriotism, the one that says, 'My country, right or wrong', and the one that asks whether the beloved country is living up to an ideal or standard of some kind. In ancient times, the only parallel is the great age of Athens. There too, men had an ideal for their country, an ideal of justice and generosity. When Athens failed to live up to this ideal, some of the greatest Athenians steadily opposed her policies, even at the risk of their lives, as with Socrates. The tragedian Euripides and the philosopher Aristotle both had to flee into exile. Aristophanes, the comic dramatist, steadily used his comedy as a criticism of the ugly policies of those in power. The historian Thucydides makes clear that the disasters that overtook Athens were a retribution for her crimes. These men did not desert Athens, any more than Jeremias deserted Jerusalem; but they did criticise her, even when her excuse was that her enemies were closing in upon her. Without a knowledge of the True God, the best of human beings can see a point of this kind.

In our own times, Germany under the Nazis offered examples of the same kind of problem. Men and women loved their country, but had an ideal of her which the Nazis were flouting. The most moving incident is that of the young students of Munich whose story is told in *Six Against Tyranny* (by Inge Scholl, trans. Cyrus Brooks, John Murray, London, 1955). But the concentration camps yielded other examples. . . . What are the rights of it all?

CHAPTER SIX

Social Revolution: The Northern Kingdom of Israel

IN THE DAYS of Solomon's son Roboam a rebel named Jeroboam won Egyptian support and formed the ten northern tribes into an independent kingdom, larger, richer and more powerful than the two-tribe kingdom of Juda-cum-Benjamin. For about two hundred years after that we have the Southern Kingdom of Juda, faithful to the House of David and spasmodically faithful to Yahweh; and the Northern Kingdom of Israel, much more given to idolatry and a prey to a series of usurpers, some of whom founded dynasties.

The longest lasting was the dynasty founded by Jehu, which ousted that founded by Achab's father Amri. Jehu was actually followed on the throne by his son, grandson and great-grandson, the last, Jeroboam II, being one of the greatest kings of either kingdom. Excavations in Samaria have shown how much he did to beautify and strengthen his capital. A little later, the Southern Kingdom of Juda also had a belated Golden Age, under Azarias, the only Hebrew king remembered also by a short form of his name, Ozias. His too was a brilliant reign.

In either case, the Book of Kings dismisses the brilliance in seven verses (4 Kings 14: 23–9; 15: 1–7), an outstanding sample of the 'prophetic' treatment of history, the assessment of human achievement from the Divine point of view. If we wish to know why the account is so curt, we have to go to the prophets Amos and Osee, who give an 'inside' picture of the long and prosperous reign of Jeroboam II (782–753 B.C.), while Michaeas and Isaias do the same for Azarias of Juda (768–740 B.C.).[1]

[1] There is more than one opinion as to the dates, especially of Azarias, who is also given as 785–734 and 786–757. The date selected comes from the chapter on Chronology in *A Catholic Commentary in Holy Scripture* (par. 125g).

HISTORICAL BACKGROUND

We need a wider context to appreciate that picture. For about five hundred years after the Israelite conquest of Chanaan under Josue (around 1250 B.C.), Western Asia was a world of small states that bickered with each other on fairly equal terms. From time to time one or another got the upper hand, first the Philistines, then David and Solomon, then the Aramaeans (a better term than Syrians). The chief Aramaean state, with its capital at Damascus, was involved in constant wars with the Northern Kingdom, Israel. The one great power, Egypt, intervened only fitfully. Everyone had forgotten that there had ever been dangerously powerful empires to the north.

And yet, from the time of Solomon (*c.* 972–931 B.C.), a people who took their name, Assyrians, from the city of Assur or Ashur on the Tigris, was deliberately preparing for world dominion—'world' of course in the sense of their known world. They were, however, ready to add to their knowledge, and in 853 B.C. the last year of the reign of Achab, they sent an exploring expedition to the Mediterranean coast. The small nations closed their ranks for a moment, but were heavily defeated at Karkar or Qarqar on the Orontes, where Achab lost all his chariots and a large contingent of infantry. This battle is known to us from Assyrian monuments, not from the Bible; but it helps us to understand why Israel was so ill-equipped in the unsuccessful wars waged, not only in the days of Achab's sons, but under the new dynasty founded by the usurper Jehu (4 Kings 13).

No one in Western Asia seems to have realised what Assyria was planning. They forgot this first attack and reverted to their quarrels with their neighbours. Even though Jehu had to pay tribute to Assyria the Bible does not record the fact.[1] This unawareness is less strange than it sounds at first, for the Assyrians were often checked by internal affairs, usurpations, attacks by other states, weak kings, an outbreak of plague (probably referred to in Amos. 6: 8–12) and so forth.

[1] It is recorded on the famous Black Stele, now in the British Museum.

Soon after Jehu's death (814 B.C.) they began to move west more definitely. Three full-scale attacks were needed before they got the better of Damascus; it was this pressure on the Aramaean states to the north that gave Israel and Juda their last Golden Age, helped by the long reigns of two able kings. Jeroboam II in particular had a most brilliant reign; in his days Samaria was a capital of which any people might be proud. He died in 753 B.C., to be followed by a trail of usurpers. In 721 B.C., the Assyrians took Samaria after a siege of three years, destroying it utterly and deporting all but the poorest of the population of the Northern Kingdom. Deportees brought in from other regions in place of the Israelites shifted the name 'Samaria' from the city to the district; they intermarried with the Israelites left behind. This mixed race came to be known as the Samaritans.

INSIDE ISRAEL

In the early part of the reign of Jeroboam II, however, nobody was bothering about Assyria. They were too busy getting rich quick. Or rather, some were getting rich while others were getting poor. Until this period of peace, the kings of Israel could not afford a discontented peasantry. They needed a high-spirited population, ready to spring to arms in defence of their farms and holdings. The solitary case of Naboth (3 Kings 21), indicates how rare it was in earlier times for a man to be dispossessed of his land; it took a staged political trial to get rid of Naboth. And the shock to public feeling was voiced by Elias, who pronounced doom on Achab because of his acquiescence. In the great days of Jeroboam II, no special jiggery-pokery was needed to get a man out of his holding; it happened too often to awaken surprise, let alone horror.

The fundamental reason was the way idolatry had sapped the moral fibre of the nation. In some ways the most startling element in the situation is that the nation of Israel was not indevout. People were assiduous in going on pilgrimage, especially to the shrines at Bethel and Dan founded by Jeroboam I, where Yahweh was worshipped under the image of a calf (3 Kings 12:

25–33). But they also frequented shrines at Galgal and Bersabee (Beersheba). Yahweh was still the official God of the nation. But the very fact that images of Him were used opened a too easy door to the worship of foreign gods and the foul rites which that involved.[1]

This religiosity did not involve any attempt to keep the Law. A particularly flagrant instance is mentioned in Amos 2: 6–8. The Law, in its concern for the poor, had laid down that a poor man's pledge to his debtor was to be returned to him before nightfall (Exod. 22: 26; Deut. 24: 10–13). The new race of moneylenders dodged this by placing the pledges in a temple, of course with the connivance of the priests; they then sold the debtors into slavery.

For side by side with the religious deterioration went the rise of a new type of rich man, no longer a man with his roots in the soil but one who could—or thought he could—sap the prosperity of the peasantry with profit to himself. First were the officials. After the immemorial custom of the East they were not paid, but were left to recoup themselves by taking more than was strictly due to the royal treasury. Rich men could bribe these officials to overlook their payment, with the result

[1] Most people have heard of the sacrificing of children to Moloch. Almost worse, and more corrupting, were what are politely called fertility cults. There is a human instinct to show the hidden powers behind the world what is wanted of them by doing it oneself. A harmless example is whistling for a wind; make wind, and perhaps the hidden powers will take the hint. But in Western Asia the hint took the form of indicating what was wanted of the gods responsible for the fertility of crops, herds and human families. The blunt name for this rite is religious prostitution. It took two forms. In the commoner variety, certain women were 'dedicated' at the shrines of fertility gods and goddesses and used for this type of prayer for the fruitfulness of fields and animals. This type is still in use in India, where the dedicated women are known as *devadasis*. In later times the cult spread into the Roman Empire. St. Paul encountered it at Corinth, and it had long been practised at Antioch in Syria. The second form was even worse; every girl before her marriage was taken and prostituted at one of these shrines as a prayer for children. Osee seems to have had this form in mind, but it was much older. These rites are the main reason for the very severe Divine judgment on the Chanaanites and Amorrhites. Even in the days of Abraham things were sliding that way—hence the reputation of Sodom for instance (Gen. 15: 16, etc). By the time of Josue these cults had corrupted not only the seaboard peoples but the Transjordan tribes akin to the Israelites, the Moabites, Ammonites and so forth. It is an ugly subject, but it is nearly impossible to understand the Old Testament unless one knows about it in outline.

that the poor had to make good the deficit in the official returns. The moneylender then came upon the scene, ending as a rule by possessing himself of the poor man's holding, and selling the owner and his family into slavery. The judges, instead of being a defence of the poor, took bribes to find in favour of the rich; while the priests, as we saw above, joined the conspiracy, doubtless for a rake-off. Last were the merchants. Trade was booming, and from the descriptions of the prophets one gathers that these were the least devout members of the community, paying not even lip-service to the demands of Yahweh. They were up to tricks, too, with weights and measures, using a big measure when buying and a small one when selling. Turn where he would, the poor man found no helper.

THE PROTEST: AMOS

One day there came to Samaria a man from Juda, a herdsman from the remote village of Thecue, out in the wilderness beyond Bethlehem. He brought with him the old Hebrew temper of the desert, a rough democracy which saw all men first and foremost in their relation to God. All through history—Moses, David, Elias, other prophets, the Baptist, St. Paul, the Desert Fathers, in our times Renan's grandson Ernest Psichari and then Charles de Foucauld—the desert has had a remarkable power of making God real to men. Out in the Judaean wilderness Amos had communed with God. And here, in the wealthy and luxurious city of Samaria, he spoke for the God he had met in the desert, the God who had given the Law from Sinai. The vivid imagery for which his book is famous is mostly drawn from his wilderness experience.

The chief point that Amos makes against the people of the Northern Kingdom is that they were all wrong about God. They claimed to worship that Yahweh who had made Himself known as HE IS to Moses out of the burning bush (Exod. 3). But the god they actually worshipped was a figment of their own minds. It is part of the greatness of Amos that he saw that this idol in the mind was even more dangerous than the material images, whether of false gods, or, more shameful, of the True God, which to us loom so big in the story. Yahweh, he insisted, would never acquiesce in this distortion of the truth about Himself. Unless they returned to God as He really is—which would involve radically altering their conduct—God would bring destruction upon them. Amos was the first in Western Asia to see what Assyria was going to mean to all that world of small states, so careless about the moral law, whether the Law of Sinai as in Israel, or the law written on the heart in the case of neighbouring peoples.

THE PROTEST CONTINUED: OSEE

Later in the reign, a good many people began to wake up to the Assyrian menace. But instead of amending their lives, one party began to court Egypt, another to try to placate Assyria (Os. 7: 11). Thus began one main point in what may be called the political platform of the prophets: the worst thing God's people could do was to look for help from Egypt. Their only hope was to trust in Yahweh—and that involved turning from their sins and keeping the Law. The clearest statement is in Isa. 30: 15. But it was the continuous witness of the prophets both before and after him, right down to the final tragedy in the days of Jeremias.

Osee, the first to make this particular point, takes over from Amos in the latter part of the reign of Jeroboam II. The king was now old and frail: his death was almost certain to lead to another usurpation, foreseen by Osee as a fitting punishment on the dynasty founded by Jehu (Os. 1: 4–5).

In general, Osee agrees with Amos in his line of denunciation, that is, his diagnosis of the situation. Yet it would be hard to find two men who differed more widely in temperament and experience. Amos with his desert background is above all the prophet of God's justice. Though he does not forget the Divine mercy, he has little hope that men will earn it in the only way possible, by repentance and amendment. Besides, as a Judan, he was speaking not exactly to his own people.

Osee by contrast was a man of Israel. His home was in the fertile, smiling region later known as Galilee. How wrong the members of the Sanhedrin were in saying that 'out of Galilee a prophet riseth not' (John 7: 52). Here he is, the prophet from Galilee, speaking to his own countrymen, heartbroken at their rejection of God's tenderness and love. True, God's love does not overlook wrongdoing, but it yearns over the wrongdoer, desiring only that he shall repent and come home.

Osee acquired this insight the hard way. His own heart had been rent by the infidelity of his beloved wife Gomer, who becomes to him the figure of faithless Israel. Just as he himself was moved to take Gomer back, after a period of purification, so too God's goodness would lead Him to take back His people, purified by the ordeal of Exile. That over, He would betroth Israel to Himself once more. . . . But as much as Amos, Osee foresaw that, unless there was a national repentance, Israel was doomed. And the instrument of the Divine doom would be Assyria.

FOR READING

1. *Amos, the Prophet of God's Justice.* Driven away from Israel by the priest of the shrine at Bethel (7: 10–17), Amos started a new type of prophetic action by committing his oracles to writing, or getting someone to do it for him. This first of the writing prophets is only one step removed from the older type who delivered their message by word of mouth. For much of his book we can follow him around as he talks to people.

Chap. 1: 1–2: 5. He gathers his audience, by a series of oracles against neighbouring peoples. This would tickle ears, yet also give lessons on God and the moral law. Then (2: 4–5), he comes closer home with an oracle against Juda.

Chap. 2: 6–4: 3. Here he comes to grips with Israel. The background is the city of Samaria. The crux comes in 3: 2; the mere fact of being God's Chosen means extra severity, not extra leniency. In 4: 1–3 the 'kine' are women, presumably ladies from one of the handsome houses come out to poke fun at the wild man from the desert. He rounds on them, much as he rounded on the priest Amasias in the passage already read. When Samaria is destroyed, these softly nurtured women will be unable to stand the rigours of the deportation. They will fall by the way before they are clear of Israelite territory at the foot of Hermon (Armon).

Chap. 4: 4–5: 27. The background is now the shrine towns, especially Bethel and Galgal. Here we find the cream of his teaching on the true nature of God. Those who sit at the gate (5: 7–12) were the judges who were perverting justice.

Chap. 6. The luxury that was making a new barrier between rich and poor. Verses 9–10 probably refer to an outbreak of plague mentioned in Assyrian records.

After chap. 6 the character of the oracles changes, which may be why the account of Amasias comes in hereabouts: these last chapters deal mainly with visions received direct from God, not with the prophet's preaching as he wandered around the country. These visions are harder to follow, and are probably better left on one side in this first reading. They are, however, punctuated by passages of a type we have already met, e.g. the doom on the merchants in 8: 4–10.

Chap. 9 sums up the message of Amos. God would punish His people, but doom would be followed by restoration. As often, restoration from Exile gives the prophet a glimpse of the Messianic Age (9: 11).

2. *Osee, the Prophet of God's Tenderness.* Chaps. 1, 2 and 3. Osee's unhappy marriage. In a fashion quite usual with prophets, he runs together the symbol and the thing symbolised. Even in a single sentence, some details may refer to his wife, some to faithless Israel.

Chaps. 6, 7, 11, 12 and 14. The rest of the book consists of loosely strung discourses put in the mouth of God Himself; here is a selection. References to fornication have a double meaning. On the one hand, idolatry is always seen in the Old Testament as a kind of inchastity, infidelity to Yahweh. On the other, there is allusion to indecent pagan rites. (See the note a few pages back, p. 53.) Bethaven (chap. 5: 8), means 'house of the idol', an ironic name for Bethel, the House of God so named after Jacob's vision of angels (Gen. 28). Ephraim was the largest and most powerful of the ten tribes of the Northern Kingdom; the name is often used as a synonym for all Israel. In 11: 4, the meaning is rather 'cords of a man'—Adam means simply 'man'—the way a humane man puts the harness on a beast so that it shall not be galled.

3. *Optional.* (a) The Book of Ruth, as a picture of another kind of rich man. Booz was the 'go'el', the kinsman whose official duty it was

to look after the affairs of an individual who for some reason fell out of the pattern of ordinary community life; e.g. it was the go'el's duty to ransom a kinsman sold into slavery. It was not usual for him to be expected to provide a dead man with an heir, but the idea could be stretched to include that also.

(b) The Book of Tobias, to remind ourselves that there were good people in the Northern Kingdom.

FOR DISCUSSION

1. What had wrong ideas of God to do with our own industrial revolution? E.g., 'You musn't mix religion and business.'

2. Is it inevitable that prosperity should lead to oppression of the poor? Our industrial revolution also came in a period of wealth and prosperity. And see Maisie Ward's *Young Mr. Newman*, pp. 224–35, for the dispossession of the peasantry. Goldsmith too, in *The Deserted Village*, warned the eighteenth century that

> '. . . a bold peasantry, its country's pride,
> If once destroyed, can never be supplied.'

For Scotland and the Highland Clearances, we are best to go to two novelists, Neil Gunn's *Butcher's Broom* and Fionn MacColla's *And the Cock Crew*.

3. What do we mean by 'repentance' in such a connection? The Bible has a good deal to say about the penance which should be an outward expression of an inward attitude. But Osee, in the first verses of chap. 6 has a passage which begins as a description of an ideal repentance, used by the Church in the Liturgy for Good Friday. Yet scholars consider that it shortly becomes an ironical account of those who thought that external penance was enough even though there was no true change of heart. The New Testament word *metanoia*, used for instance by the Baptist, means in Greek 'change of mind', in our idiom perhaps rather a new scale of values, a new outlook, a new way of seeing things.

4. Has the lack of a wide-scale 'change of mind' played any part among ourselves? Could it be said that the modern 'prophetical' warning was, e.g., Leo XIII's encyclical on *Capital and Labour*? If that had been acted on at once, on a sufficiently wide scale, there might have been no Communist revolution, or at least one on a more manageable scale. Yet in France some Catholic industrialists did their best to prevent its being read in churches. And more recently in connection with the Spanish civil war, it has been said that the

chief obstacle to Christian social reform in the years preceding it were certain landowners whose line was: 'We are not going to have the Pope tell us what to do about our property.'

5. Would you agree with the simple Spaniard who, after listening to long discussions on the social changes needed in his country, said thoughtfully: 'All it means is that everybody should keep the Ten Commandments'?

CHAPTER SEVEN

Social Revolution: The Southern Kingdom of Juda

NO SITUATION ever stands still. While the social revolution followed much the same course in Juda as in Israel, the world background was markedly different. True, we begin with the long and brilliant reign of Azarias (Ozias for short), which overlapped with the last fifteen years of Jeroboam II of Israel; this phase of (apparent) peace and prosperity carried over into the reign of Azarias' son Joatham or Joathan, and into the early years of his grandson Achaz. Yet even in that apparently peaceful phase Assyria was making itself felt in the north, and before the end of the reign of Achaz Assyria was mistress of Western Asia as far south as, and including, Israel.

GENERAL SITUATION

That is to say, the people of Juda saw the doom pronounced by Amos and Osee actually carried out, almost under their eyes. They were genuinely scared, and with reason; Assyria was the most cruel of the ancient empires, indeed was hardly an empire in the sense of an organised government. Its one interest was loot, hence the huge tributes exacted from conquered states. In their terror, the people of Juda turned more and more to such professional prophets as would say what everyone wanted to hear: that Assyria would never be allowed to destroy the Temple in Jerusalem, or that God could be appeased by bigger sacrifices without change of conduct.

It is in this phase that we begin to hear constantly about false prophets. Those prophets who catered for wishful thinking had a large share in the worst feature of the situation: with Israel going the way Amos and Osee had foretold, Juda went on doing the things against which her neighbour had been warned, pinching the poor out of their holdings, perverting justice, running after foreign gods, and imagining that so long as Yahweh got His due in the way of cultus He had no right to question men's morals.

And then two things happened. In the first place, the doom threatened by Amos and Osee was fulfilled, almost under the eyes of the people of Juda. Yet that alone might not have been enough. Three years before the Assyrians laid siege to Samaria, there came to the throne of Juda the young Ezechias, a man with a genuinely new attitude and scale of values, that inner change which the New Testament calls *metanoia*. Under the influence of Isaias, helped too, no doubt, by the shock to public feeling of the siege and capture of Samaria and the deportation that followed it, Ezechias carried out a thorough reform of religious practices, putting down idolatry and restoring the pure worship of Yahweh. And this change of heart, supported by the better sort throughout the nation, is the reason why the people of Juda were deported, not by Sennacherib of Assyria, but a hundred and fifty years later by Nabuchodonosor of Babylon. Such is the power of genuine repentance.

As with the Northern Kingdom, we have to go to two prophets to get an 'inside' picture of what was happening. One of them, Michaeas, was a countryman; his little book makes it clear that the reform of Ezechias was not as successful out in the country as it was in Jerusalem under the king's eye. The other, by contrast, was a member of the aristocracy, Isaias, with his home in Jerusalem. His outlook was in some ways more 'political' than that of Michaeas. In particular he carried on Osee's work in resisting the tendency to expect help from Egypt; that he called 'entering into a league with death, making a covenant with hell'—i.e. Sheol, the underworld of the dead (Isa. 28: 15). Yet at the same time he is supremely 'the evangelical prophet' or 'prophet of the Gospel', the one who in all the Old Testament comes closest to the message of pardon and love in the New.

PERSONALITIES AND EVENTS

Both prophets need to be seen against the background of events, of which the main history is given in 4 Kings 15–21 and 2 Par. 26–32. The Chronicler—such is the accepted short way of saying 'the anonymous author of Paralipomenon'—fills in a number of personal details, and only mentions the Northern Kingdom when its affairs touched Juda. And Assyrian inscriptions, deciphered by the archaeologists, often supplement the Biblical account in a way that makes it easier to seize the main points. The story thus pieced together is best taken reign by reign:

1. *Azarias.* This mainly good king, with a mainly good religious policy, did one terrible thing: he allowed his successes to go to his head so that he insisted on offering incense in the Temple, a duty reserved to priests. For this presumption he was stricken with leprosy.

His son *Joathan* or *Joatham* is best taken along with his father. Oriental fashion, he was associated in the kingship with his father, to carry on public business after Azarias' leprosy drove him from public life. It is not important to be sure when Joathan became sole king; he continued his father's mainly good religious policy and the country continued to enjoy its phase of prosperity.

2. *Achaz.* With Joathan's son Achaz the scene begins to change, both within and without. Of all the kings of Juda, Achaz seems to have been the one most given to experimenting with new gods. It may have been sheer terror that made him hunt around for a deity who would protect him from the gathering perils (without the tiresome necessity for amending his life, though that was probably not put plainly into words). He introduced, or reintroduced, the burning alive of children in sacrifice to Moloch. This rite was carried out in the valley south-east of Jerusalem, called the valley of Ben-Ennom or Gehenna, where the city's rubbish was incinerated in a great burning-pit called a *tephet* or *tophet.*

It is quite possible that all through Western Asia there was just then a tendency to turn to the more dreadful kind of rites. With the Assyrian menace hanging over them, there was a feeling that the dark powers behind the course of events were the ones most needing to be bought off by the most horrible rites that could be devised. Besides its cruelty, then, this cultus of Moloch pointed to a fundamental want of faith in Yahweh as the Lord and Ruler of history, and for both reasons the prophets fiercely loathed it.

These inside changes were thus a response to the changing political situation throughout Western Asia. In the first place, Israel was having a whole series of usurpations, as Osee had foreseen. Usurpers arose so often that Assyrian recorders seem to have lost track of them and put down payments of tribute to the last name they could remember.

Nor was Israel alone in being troubled with usurpers. About the time that Achaz became king of Juda (736 B.C.) a certain Phul or Pulu seized the throne of Assyria and took the ancient kingly name of Tiglath Pileser or Theglath Philassar; the Bible sometimes uses the old name, sometimes the new. Now, in ancient times a new reign was often a good chance for successful revolt. The Mediterranean countries, writhing under the heavy tribute exacted from them, thought this a good moment to try to shake off the Assyrian yoke. The Israelite usurper of the moment, Phacee son of Romelia, joined the confederacy. He and Rasin king of Damascus then tried to get Achaz to join too, though at that time Juda was not a tributary of Assyria. Achaz had enough sense to refuse, whereupon Phacee and Rasin attacked Jerusalem, announcing their intention of deposing him in favour of a nominee of their own.

Achaz thereupon lost his head, in spite of all Isaias could say to reassure him: Had not God promised the throne of Juda to the line of David for ever? The famous prophecy of Emmanuel was uttered at this juncture, a striking sample of the way Messianic prophecy often grew out of a contemporary situation (Isa. 7: 1–16). But Achaz would not listen. He rushed off to bribe Tiglath Pileser with an offer of money if he would invade Israel. The Assyrian king pocketed the cash, quite pleased to be paid for doing what he was going to do in any case, and wrote off the king of Juda not as an ally but as a tributary. Tiglath Pileser then crushed the revolt, killed Rasin of Damascus, and in Israel put in his own nominee, a puppet-king called Osee who had nothing in common with the prophet Osee save the name.

3. *Ezechias.* Achaz and Tiglath Pileser died at about the same time in 727 B.C. In Juda this brought to the throne the reforming king Ezechias, whose first big political decision was brought on by a new move from Egypt. In the Nile delta there was a military commander, not strictly an Egyptian but a Kushite (Ethiopian), from the remote region we now call the Sudan. This vigorous personality is variously called So (pronounced Sēwē) or Shua, on his own monuments Sabaka or Shabaka, for he later became Pharao and the founder of a Kushite dynasty. On the death of Tiglath Pileser he played the traditional Egyptian game, instigating the small states to rebellion. On this occasion Isaias managed to persuade Ezechias to keep out of trouble. But Osee of Israel joined the revolt, soon crushed by the new king of Assyria, Shalmaneser V. It was Shalmaneser who laid siege to Samaria, but he died before taking it. Hence it was his successor, the great Sargon II, who captured and destroyed it after a siege of three years. In 721 B.C. the end came, and almost all the inhabitants of the Northern Kingdom were deported (4 Kings 17). Israel as a state ceased to exist. And the prophets in Juda soon ceased to keep the name Israel for the ten tribes only; they reverted to its original meaning, the whole Chosen People descended from Abraham's grandson Jacob, also called Israel.

At this point, there was only one state left in Western Asia that was to any degree independent, the smallest and weakest of all, Juda. Now, Ezechias was willing to listen to prophets about religion, but when it came to politics he was apt to grow restive. On the death of Sargon II a new reign in Assyria once again invited revolt, and in Babylon a man called Merodach Baladan took advantage of it to set up a short-lived independent state. Ezechias gave an unwisely warm welcome to his ambassadors (4 Kings 20: 12 ff.; Isa. 39).

The same new reign, that of Sennacherib, inspired Egypt to start its old games once more, inciting the small peoples to revolt. Most of them responded. One of the Philistine cities deposed its puppet-king, nominated by the Assyrians, and Ezechias allowed him to be imprisoned in Jerusalem. It was not a very big act of rebellion, but quite enough to bring Assyria down on him. So it came that when Sennacherib stormed south in 701 B.C. his reckoning with Egypt included a reckoning with Hazakiau-Yaudaa, Ezechias the Jew. This is the background of one of the great deliverance stories of the Old Testament (4 Kings 18 and 19; Isa. 36 and 37. Tartan or Tharthan is the Assyrian word for a commander-in-chief).

ISAIAS

All of this helps us to understand the role of Isaias. He received his call to the prophetic office in the last year of Ozias, i.e. Azarias, and was at work through the reigns of Joathan and Achaz. Scholars think that in the last years of Achaz he may have gone into retirement, feeling that he could do more good by training disciples than by presence at court. For there always were disciples of the prophets; we hear so much of their opponents that it is important to remind ourselves of their faithful following. When Ezechias came to the throne Isaias had his big opportunity. But in the next reign, that of Manasses, there was a swing back to the evil ways of Achaz, with even more violence. Jewish tradition, echoed in the Epistle to the Hebrews (11: 37) has it that Isaias was murdered by order of Manasses. . . . Perhaps our best farewell to this great and lovable prophet is his chapter 26: 1–12.

In the midst of such exciting events it may seem surprising that anyone had time to worry about the oppression of the poor. One mark of the greatness of the prophets, their independence of ordinary human standards, is their refusal to be carried away by the general excitement. They kept a clear eye for what would earn God's blessing, or His doom. The prosperity which had begun under Azarias lasted into the early years of his grandson

Achaz, when it was wrecked by the joint attack of Israel and Damascus on Jerusalem. After that life became harder for everybody. The prophets' criticisms may alter a little in detail; but in good or ill fortune they stuck to their message: Let men only obey God, both in His cult Laws and His moral Law, and He would see to it that they were safe from their enemies.

FOR READING

1. *Michaeas*. Chapters 1, 2 and 3 give the main points of his social criticism. In chapters 4 and 5 we have a background of war with one of the most famous Messianic prophecies (5: 2) embedded in it.

In chapter 6 the prophet stages a trial scene, with God as judge, himself as advocate, and Israel (the whole Chosen People) as his client. The common people were genuinely puzzled as to what the prophets were driving at. At this period they were not taught the Law; that was taken in hand systematically only after the Return from Babylon. In the Monarchy period, they trusted to custom and the lead given by their rulers, often a very bad lead. A good lead, such as that given by Ezechias, seemed to them just one more royal vagary.

In the trial scene, the prophet first summoned all nature to witness to God's goodness to His ungrateful people (6: 1, 2). God then pleads with them, the first seeds of the Improperia of Good Friday (verses 3–5a). The people (verses 6–7), are half puzzled, half amused. What *is* the fuss all about? Have they ever stinted Yahweh of His cult dues? Why, they are willing to increase those to fantastic amounts. They are even willing to sacrifice their children to Him instead of to Moloch (the latter part of verse 7). At this appalling suggestion the prophet breaks in: What God wants of them is something quite simple. Not all these gifts and sacrifices, but right conduct, especially justice, mercy, and a humble 'walk' with God as their Friend. In verses 8–16 God tell them plainly what He finds amiss. Yet at the very end of the book (7: 18–20) is a word of mercy. Verse 18 is almost a pun on the name Michaeas. For as Micha-el means Who is like God (El)? so Micha-iah means Who is like Yahweh?

2. *Isaias*. We must not think of the prophet as sitting down to write a book. He uttered oracles, which either he or a friend afterwards recorded. Copies then circulated from hand to hand in quite small sheets. Later, these were collected and arranged in the order

which has come down to us, the editors adding notes of dates and suchlike.

(a) *Azarias, Joathan, Early Years of Achaz.* Chapter 1. Like the Northern Kingdom, Juda was prone to think that ritual observance dispensed from keeping the moral law (verses 11–14).

Chapter 2. Evil-doing (verses 1–9) would lead to a manifestation of God's anger.

Chapter 3. In 1–5 the details may have been suggested by what, was actually happening in the Northern Kingdom at that moment: Juda would share the fate of Israel if she did not repent and amend. In verse 3, the 'skilful' are probably magicians, and in verse 12 'women' is more probably 'usurers'. Note verse 15, Isaias' most famous bit of social criticism. Verses 16–24, an oracle against the fashionable ladies; apparently they wore tiny chains between their ankles to ensure taking only daintily short steps.

Chapter 5. The Vineyard.

(b) *Achaz: the War with Israel and Damascus.* Chapters 7 and 8.

(c) *Ezechias: Assyria invades the Northern Kingdom.* Chapter 9. The great Messianic prophecy of verses 6–8 had for background the Assyrian invasion of what was later Galilee (Zabulon, Nephthali). Juda would meantime be safe under its good king Ezechias (verse 7) who thus becomes a symbol of the Messias.

(d) *Ezechias: Juda threatened by Sennacherib.* Chapter 10. Juda has deserved chastisement as much as Israel (1–4); but the prophet sees further, to pardon and peace (20–27). In verses 28–32 he seems to be standing on the city wall watching the burning townships to the north as the Assyrian army comes up from the Coastal Plain. Verse 24 has been called 'one of the bravest utterances ever made'. In chapter 11, the deliverance from Sennacherib grows into a vision of the Messianic Age.

(e) *Isaias on Egypt.* Chapter 18. Somebody had told the prophet about the flies that infest the Nile, and about the reed boats of the Sudan. The Kushite Pharao Shabaka (Shua, So) tried to involve Ezechias in revolt against Assyria (verse 2) and succeeded with surrounding states. Isaias here insists that Juda is to await a signal that Assyria has been defeated (verse 6); after that Kush (Ethiopia) will send a thankoffering to the shrine of Yahweh in Jerusalem. Chapter 19 is an oracle against not Kush but the real Egypt; she will be defeated by Assyria, a fate as dreadful as the drying up of her irrigation canals (rivers, verse 6). But in the Messianic Age (verses 16–25)

Egypt will be converted to Yahweh. Even more (verses 22–4) there will be a conversion of Assyria as well, after which there will be friendship between these former enemies.

(f) *God's Judgment of All Nations.* The prophets always saw Yahweh as the Judge of the Whole Earth (Gen. 18: 25). He would deal specially severely with His chosen people, with others according to the light they had, the natural moral law written on the heart (chap. 34).

(g) *God's Pardon and Mercy.* Chapter 35.

FOR DISCUSSION

1. If the Northern Kingdom under Jeroboam II was suggestive of the prosperous nineteenth century, this later phase is closer to our twentieth century with its background of menace and disaster. What is the duty of those who would serve God in social matters in the face of catastrophe that looks like sweeping away all their labours? What encouragement is there in the reminder that God has seen the world through periods of breakdown before now?

2. How far is the element of repentance, then deliverance, affected by the fact that we have here God's central dealings with the human race? What was at issue was not just Juda and Israel, but God's providence and promises for all mankind. We ourselves felt over Dunkirk that God came to our help because all mankind was affected by the issues between the West and the Nazis; even an anti-Nazi German could have the same feeling (Theodor Haecker in his *Journal in the Night*) not in afterthought but at the time. There was here a touch of the Old Testament, but what are the resemblances, what the differences?

3. What difference is made by the fact that we live not under the Old Law but under the New? The Old Testament has little to say about individual responsibility until we come to Jeremias, still more to Ezechiel, and that was a century and a half after Isaias. Its unit of responsibility is the nation or community. How far is this principle still valid? Up to a point, we can see that nations tend to create their own disasters. But we can hardly urge that the Iron Curtain countries were particularly wicked. Poland, Czecho-Slovakia and Hungary had a better record of social justice than ourselves. Have the Poles picked up a real point in seeing their country as 'the Messias-Nation', with a special vocation to suffer for Christendom?

CHAPTER EIGHT

The Revolution Wrought by Iron

THROUGH MOST of the Old Testament, iron is spoken of in something the tone that creeps into our voices at the mention of uranium or tungsten. It was the new metal which gave its possessors a decisive advantage in both tools and armaments. It came into general use only slowly, because every people that got hold of it tried to keep the smelting process a secret. Even if they sold the finished product, it was at fabulous prices. At the time when iron becomes important in the Old Testament story, when the Israelites under Josue were making their assault on Chanaan, around 1250 B.C., iron objects were nearly as costly as those made of gold and silver. A king who could afford to have his chariots armoured with iron was a very wealthy man.

To get the picture we have to go back. As far as Western Asia is concerned, iron seems to have been worked in the Caucasus before 3000 B.C. We need not trouble our heads with such a remote period, because the story keeps repeating itself; one people after another tried to keep the new metal for itself. We can take a jump and begin in the days of the Patriarchs, around 1900–1700 B.C., when an Aryan people calling themselves the Khatti began to work iron in Asia Minor, and with its aid disputed with Egypt for the control of our present Syria and Palestine. They appear in the Bible as the Hethites or Hittites. On their withdrawal, a considerable sprinkling of them seems to have been left behind in the lands they once conquered. Abraham bought his burial-cave from a Hethite (Gen. 23). Almost a thousand years later, in the time of King David, the husband of Bethsabee was a Hethite, Urias (2 Kings 11 and 12). If Bethsabee was also a Hethite, then Our Lord ultimately had in His veins some drops of Khatti blood.[1]

[1] His ancestors were of course all from the Chosen People. But his ancestresses were slightly more varied, including Rahab of Jericho, Ruth the Moabitess, and Bethsabee.

INVADERS OF PALESTINE

To resume our main thread: while the Israelites were in Egypt, before the time of Moses, the Khatti lost the secret of iron-smelting to those whom the Egyptians called the Sea Peoples, the inhabitants of the Mediterranean islands and coastlands. How this happened is not clear. A possible guess is that the Khatti employed prisoners of war in their mines and that some of them escaped with the secret. The Sea Peoples, however, had no time to do very much about it. Before they could cash in on their new knowledge, a wave of invaders swept down from what is now Southern Russia and pushed them out of their homes. They took to their ships, the largest contingent apparently coming from Crete, called in Hebrew Caphtor (Amos 9: 7). They first tried to land in Egypt, but were beaten off in a battle vividly depicted by an Egyptian artist. The Sea Peoples then rowed up the coast and landed where the desert ends at the southern end of the Palestine Coastal Plain. There they made their settlements, five cities each under its separate ruler. Gaza and Geth were their chief cities, and ultimately they gave their name to the whole country: Palestine means the land of the Philistines.

This was around 1200 B.C. and they were by no means the only incomers. The Hebrews were already pushing up into the Central Plateau from east of Jordan. And a third people, the Aramaeans—a better name than Syrians—were coming down from the north. They are not mentioned in the Bible until later, because at this early phase they were busy pushing out those of the Chanaanites who lived east of the Lebanon ranges. These dispossessed groups moved through the mountain passes to the sea coast where they became the chief seafaring people of antiquity, the Phoenicians, operating from the great harbour of Tyre. In the territory the Phoenicians had vacated the Aramaeans set up a group of kingdoms, the chief with its capital at Damascus. Later, they were in frequent conflict with the kings of Israel.

While this was going on in the north, the Philistines and the

Hebrews were contending for control of the country between the Jordan Valley and the sea coast. They sometimes destroyed, sometimes made terms with, the older inhabitants of the land, variously called Chanaanites or Amorrhites. Both these older groups practised a particularly vile type of idolatry. So did the Phoenicians who settled on the coast along the foot of the Lebanon, but they did not begin to contaminate the Israelites until a good deal later.

ISRAELITE CONQUEST AND SETTLEMENTS

It is now that iron begins to come into the Bible story. The archaeologists have established that the Hebrews entered Palestine just as the Late Bronze Age was yielding to the Early Iron Age. Weapons were still mostly of bronze, because iron weapons had to be bought from the Khatti at fancy prices. Humanly speaking, the Hebrews failed to make a complete conquest because they could not cope with a sort of tank corps—iron-armed chariots—when their weapons were only swords, and bronze swords at that. God had promised them victory, even over the iron chariots (Jos. 17: 14–18; Judges 1: 19) if they kept His Law. They broke their side of the Covenant, hence were left to experience the natural consequences of fighting peoples with a more modern and powerful type of armament.

Archaeology spells out the story. Jericho for instance is one of the oldest settlements in the world; in the warmth of the deep Jordan valley, at that point a mile below Mediterranean level, men could live before they had gained full control of fire; and it was the control of fire that opened the way to every other civilised achievement, cooking, pottery, metal-working. Every new invader, every new culture, built a town at Jericho, watching the fords of Jordan on one side and the passes up to the plateau on the other. Jericho is thus the spot where the continuous development of early cultures can best be traced. Now, the city which Josue took and destroyed belonged to the Late Bronze Age; that city came down in an earthquake and was burned by fire (Jos. 5 and 6). But the first all-Israelite settlement up on the plateau is an Early Iron Age township, Silo, the place where the Tabernacle was given its home (Jos. 18: 1, 8). Silo continued the religious centre of the Israelites down to the time of Samuel, who was brought up in the sanctuary there (1 Kings 1, 2 and 3). At some period it was destroyed, presumably by the Philistines (Ps. 77: 60). Later, in the time of Jeremias and Ezechiel, when the superstition arose that Yahweh would never allow His Temple in Jerusalem to be destroyed, Jeremias twice pointed out that the fate of Silo was a warning (Jer. 7: 12, 14; 26: 6, 9). These oblique allusions are our only information about the city's end. The excavated site shows that Silo was not very long-lived as cities go.

IRON AND ISRAEL'S ENEMIES

As the Bible story goes on we have to read somewhat between the lines. It looks as if the Philistines were not immediately able to exploit their knowledge of iron-smelting. There is no iron-ore in Palestine proper. But there is, or was, in Transjordan, and it is these deposits that are probably meant in Deut 8: 9. Significantly, we first meet the Philistines as the allies of a Transjordan people, the Ammonites, whose country was rich in iron; in this first account (Judges 10: 6 ff.) it looks as if the Philistines were the subordinate partner. The suggestion would seem to be that the Philistines and the Ammonites did a deal, the Ammonites supplying the iron ore from which the Philistines manufactured arms for their allies as well as for themselves. Before long, however, the Philistines had no need of Ammonite support in dealing with Israel; by the time of Samson they are obviously the chief local power. And west of Jordan at least they had a monopoly of iron.

The Philistine onslaught forced the Hebrew tribes to unite, setting up a monarchy on the pattern normal at the period, in order to secure a unified command in war. One problem for the first king of Israel, Saul, was the way the Philistines had contrived to keep all iron-working in their own hands; even the most necessary tools had to be taken to their cities for sharpening

(1 Kings 13: 19–22). In that passage, it looks as if the word 'sword' now meant 'iron sword'. We are told that only Saul and Jonathan had swords, yet the Philistines could hardly have removed all the bronze swords which the Israelites had owned in the time of Josue; it is rather that bronze swords hardly counted as weapons, any more than we should consider muzzle-loaders a serious item in military equipment to-day.

This underlines Jonathan's generosity to David, giving him not only his princely robes but his sword (1 Kings 18: 4 ff.). The account of Goliath's armour carries the same suggestion. His body armour was of bronze, and we are specifically told that his spearhead was of iron (17: 4–7). But the metal of which his sword was made is not mentioned; apparently the word 'sword' was enough by itself. No wonder David was so keen to get hold of Goliath's sword when he had to flee from the hatred of Saul (1 Kings 21: 1–9).

THE ISRAELITES GET HOLD OF IRON

That flight ultimately made David a refugee among the Philistines. Is it too much to suggest that this sojourn opened his eyes to the importance of cutting the Philistines off from their supplies of iron ore and diverting the ore to himself? Possibly, too, he or his companions did a little snooping and learned more about iron-smelting than the Philistines would have wished. At any rate, once David was securely on the throne, one of his first acts was to make war on the Ammonites. The Bible tells the story in terms of personal collisions (2 Kings 10, 11 and 12), but it is quite common for people not to see clearly the nature of the revolution through which they are living. The final words of chapter 12 are thought to be a brutal way of saying that David forced the Ammonites to work their iron-mines for his advantage, as well as their brick-kilns. At any rate, the Hebrew monarchy now had iron at its disposal. The mines actually found in Transjordan are of Solomon's reign; they have a remarkably efficient system of blast furnaces.

The person who gives us a clue to the difference which this

was to make is the prophet Samuel. He was all along opposed to the idea of setting up a king, and annointed Saul only in obedience to a direct Divine command (1 Kings 8 and 9). In his first effort to dissuade the people he dwells on what were then normal methods by which government was carried on. The king would take toll both of their goods and of their sons. Among his needs would be men to fight, to drive chariots, and to make armour.

The reference is quite casual, one item among many. Yet this particular item, the royal control of the armoury, was to alter the relation of ruler and ruled, much as the invention of gunpowder did at the end of our own Middle Ages. Among us, it was gunpowder that made possible the standing army, since only the government could afford the new weapons. And the standing army made possible the absolute monarchy. So with iron. By becoming, inevitably, a royal monopoly, it put an end to the old comradeship of the desert, a spirit more or less democratic, which the Israelites had brought from Sinai and which made a man first and foremost a man.

In the end, royal exactions became such a problem that as late as the Exile in Babylon we find the prophet Ezechiel giving thought to the matter. The remedy he suggested was that monarchy should be endowed, which was in fact the principle of Medieval Europe. 'The King should live of his own', said the Parliament of Perth, even to Robert the Bruce, and even when voting him a subsidy of every twelfth penny in consideration of his extra expenses in liberating the country. The extra help was necessary, but it was not to be a precedent. Among the Jews, the principle was never acted on, because the monarchy was not restored after the Return from Babylon. But it is arresting that Ezechiel should have thought of it (Ezech. 45: 7–8; 46: 16–18).

THE TRADE IN METALS

In a way, that is the end of the story. But we may see its significance more clearly if we look at the trade of the ancient world. An immense amount of that trade was concerned with the quest for metals. Copper came first; an island where it was early found gives most languages their word for copper, Cyprus. Then it was discovered that a mixture of tin with copper gave a much stronger amalgam, which we call bronze. The quest for metals was thus enlarged to include tin. Gold and silver were early in demand both for ornament and for money.

As far as the Old Testament is concerned, the story is mainly that of the Phoenicians, whom we mentioned earlier. Their ships went out from Tyre and Sidon on a very thorough exploration of the resources of the Mediterranean area. Wherever they made a find they set up a smelting-post, in their language a *tharsis* or *tarshish*. Some of these smelting-posts grew into cities, possibly St. Paul's Tarsus, certainly the port later called Tarsessus in Spain. This Spanish *tharsis* was to the Jews the extreme western limit of the world (Jonas 1: 3). The Phoenicians, however, did not bother about limits. In course of time their ships nosed their way past the Pillars of Hercules into the Atlantic. And there they discovered a rich source of tin, called by the Greeks the Cassiterides, the Tin Islands, either the Scillies or possibly Cornwall itself.

Nor did they confine themselves to the Mediterranean. They pushed down the Red Sea and had a smelting-post somewhere in eastern waters; this *tharsis* seems to have specialised in gold and silver (3 Kings 10: 22). Incidentally, in that verse the word for 'peacocks' comes from a South Indian language, Tamil. Whether Solomon's ships went so far, or whether the Jews picked up the word from the Phoenicians, it gives some idea of how enterprising that ancient commerce was. Ezechiel gives the fullest list of metals which interested the Phoenicians: silver and iron, tin and lead (Ezech. 27: 12). Nearly every mention of Tyre and Tharsis includes some allusion to metals.

Solomon, it may be remembered, was friendly with the king of Tyre, Hiram, from whom he borrowed a craftsman, also called Hiram, to make the ornaments for his own palace (3 Kings 7: 13 ff.). Hiram the king was moreover friendly and helpful over Solomon's own trading ventures, lending ships and shipbuilders (3 Kings 9: 26–8). But the archaeologists have filled in a detail. On the Gulf of Akaba, the eastern branch of the Red Sea at its northern end, they have found a building which was apparently both a fort and a factory. It is of Solomon's period, and appears to be the place where the goods for his oriental trade were manufactured. They seem to have consisted mainly of bronze articles, for bronze continued in demand for ornamental purposes long after it was out-dated as a material for tools or weapons. Neither Solomon nor Hiram was going to export anything so modern and up-to-date as iron. They wanted all the iron they could get for themselves.

. . . Is all this really in the Bible? Well, the general background of world-history has been worked out by the archaeologists. But the effect is to give many details mentioned in the Bible a new and sharper point. Every age sees in the Bible what is relevant to its own concerns. Such is the richness of the Word of God. In our age, God's providence has raised up the archaeologists to give us the sort of economic 'slant' which most comes home to us, and with that some rather direct probing of twentieth-century consciences.

FOR READING

The best thing seems to be to suggest fairly wide-sweeping reading in the historical books, leaving each reader to do his own skipping, using the information given above as his background. Observe that those who live through a major economic revolution rarely notice what is happening.

1. *The Beginnings of Metal-Working*. The Bible places all the major discoveries on which civilisation is based in the line of Cain: Gen. 4: 16 ff. In verse 22 the mention of iron does not mean that it was discovered so early. The regular plan in Genesis is to bring a side-issue—and the line of Cain is a side-issue—right down to the times of Moses when, as said above, iron began to be an important factor in Western Asia. In verses 23–4, the Song of Lamech is thought to refer to the new deadliness of killing when men had metal weapons.

2. *The Conquest of Chanaan*, which took place just as the Late Bronze Age was yielding to the Early Iron Age. Jos. 1–6; 7–11. (For Rahab, see Matt. 1: 5, also James 2: 25.)

3. *The Philistines*. Judges 10: 6 ff. The story of Samson, Judges

13–16. The Book of Judges has two main objects: (a) to rub in the lesson that infidelity to God leads to disaster. It makes no attempt to whitewash the doings of the Chosen People. God kept His side of the Covenant, both in mercy and chastisement, even though they constantly broke theirs. (b) To serve as propaganda for the idea of the monarchy. Until there was a central government to enforce the Law it would never be kept. As so often happens in human affairs, the monarchy did not come up to expectations. Samuel, as we saw, was opposed to the idea of the monarchy—one more instance of the way the Bible looks at events from more than one point of view.

4. *Samuel*, last of the judges, 1 Kings 1–8.

5. *Saul, the First King*. 1 Kings 9–31. In chapter 13: 1 the Septuagint, a Greek translation made about 250 B.C., gives Saul's age as thirty. In chapter 15: 33 the hewing in pieces is probably an exaggeration. During the Exile in Babylon the Jews ceased to speak Hebrew, so a good deal of the Old Testament was paraphrased for reading in the newly adopted language, Aramaic. In several places these *targums* (translations) give a more bloodthirsty account of what happened than the Hebrew Bible; in this instance, and some others, it is probable that the targum exaggerations were copied by scribes into the Hebrew text.

6. *The Reign of David*. 2 Kings 1 to the end of 3 Kings 2. The story is a remarkable instance of the 'prophetic' treatment of history. David was a great and good king, rightly remembered with love and veneration. But he had one great weakness, sensuality. He got to the point of thinking he was entitled to have any woman who took his fancy. The historian treats the episode of Bethsabee and Urias as the turning-point of his reign. Incidentally, the various rebellions (2 Kings 13–14 and 16–18) are also fruits of his sensuality. The moral comment is in the story itself.

7. *The Reign of Solomon*. 3 Kings 3–11. The best omissions are chapters 4 and 7.

FOR DISCUSSION

1. The whole chapter really gives the subject. What are the rights and wrongs of trying to keep new discoveries for ourselves? Obviously the question is no new one; but the publicity which everything receives nowadays gives the matter a new urgency.

2. If the kings of Israel and Juda had really kept the Law, and

'maintained' it, would the consequences of the economic revolution have been what they actually were?

3. Can you think of any modern revolutions which passed unnoticed until they were so firmly in the saddle that they had to be accepted? If the generations that in actual fact saw the beginnings of industrialism, and the land enclosures, had been on the watch to apply Christian principles in economic life, what difference would it have made?

CHAPTER NINE

Piecing the Cosmos Together: Creation Stories in the Old Testament

TO MAKE CLEAR what we propose to talk about: there is only one Biblical *doctrine* of Creation, but there is more than one story or picture or account. The doctrine, of course, is that God made out of nothing all that is, and that He keeps complete control of what He thus made. But this truth is beyond our power to make pictures of, whereas most human beings are stronger on the side of imagination than of thought. In the Old Testament, therefore, we find God inspiring the Hebrew poets to give various pictures of God at work creating the world. The most-discussed one, the prose-poem with which the Book of Genesis opens, has more in common with poetic imagination than with abstract thought. But it is not the only picture-treatment of the subject. And it helps to an appreciation of this greatest account if we have some familiarity with the others.

Broadly speaking, so long as a poet taught the doctrine, he seems to have had considerable liberty in his treatment of his picture or story. In one sense, only Genesis is an account, an orderly presentation of the activity of God in creating. In the others, each poet followed his individual tastes, picking out details that specially appealed to himself. Creation always seems to have warmed a Hebrew imagination. What enthralled all the poets was God's handling of water.

THE GOD OF ISRAEL

All peoples, of course, told stories of how their gods made the world. What largely conditioned the story was the kind of god or gods concerned. Naturally, then, the Hebrew stories are conditioned from beginning to end by the character of the God of Israel.

Israel's God differed from other gods in three main ways: He was the Author, not the representative or manifestation, of nature; He was the Author of the Moral Law; and He was the Ruler and Director of history, guiding the course of events to bring about the ends He had chosen. When then any spokesman for God was trying to recall his fellow-countrymen from running after false gods, these were the points he would stress. He did not necessarily stick to any one of them, but jumped from one to the other and back again. Hence creation, though often mentioned, is seldom isolated and treated by itself for its own interest; it is constantly intertwined with the two other themes, the Law, and God's control of history. Possibly in reading Amos, it was noticed how the prophet's thoughts on creation stab suddenly through his treatment of other motifs (Amos. 4: 12–13; 5: 8; 9: 5–6).

THE ANCIENT WORLD-PICTURE

These Hebrew picture-stories or accounts have one feature in common: they all take for granted what was in those days the best scientific view of how the cosmos fitted together. They do not exactly teach this ancient cosmology, but they do assume it. The Hebrews were not one of the scientific peoples of the ancient world; they were content to take over the general world-view worked out in Babylon and Egypt, later in Greece. To enjoy their picture-stories, we need some idea of what this ancient world-view was.

In this ancient cosmology, the earth was a flat disc floating on an abyss of water. This abyss, the depth or great deep, became visible in the sea, and it clearly extended under the earth, since everywhere springs rose up to flow away in streams and rivers. That is why the Hebrews do not seem to draw a very marked distinction between salt water and fresh; it was all part of the great deep. Hence at one moment leviathan seems to be the whale, at another the crocodile. In either case, the word 'leviathan' was originally applied to a mythological monster; only by degrees was it used of real creatures, and there was not always complete agreement as to what animal was meant—much turned on what was the most exciting creature the individual poet had seen or heard of. In Ps. 73: 13 and Ps. 103: 26 the dragon—leviathan—lives in the sea. In Job 40: 20, the literal meaning is 'Canst thou draw out leviathan with a hook?' and the description that follows is much more like a crocodile than a whale. There are instances in which leviathan, the serpent or dragon, is used in the original mythological meaning of a monster, as in Job 3: 8. And in Isa. 27: 1 it applied metaphorically to a king of Assyria. All of which is a reminder of the play allowed to poetic fancy.

To get back to our cosmology. Round the rim of the great earth-disc floating on the abyss was a circle of mountains. If we look at a map of the Old Testament world, we can easily see that in several directions it ends in a mountain barrier, the Caucasus, Armenia, further east on the borders of India. Similarly, the Nile valley is closed in on the west by a fairly high mountain chain, and on the south by the Abyssinian highlands. The mountains forming this rim were spoken of as the 'pillars', since they were regarded as the supports holding up the overarching dome of sky (Job 9: 6; 26: 11; Ps. 74: 3).

So we come to the sky or firmament. In hot countries it *looks* solid, both by day and by night, in quite a different way from our soft, cloudy northern skies; in seeing it as a dome or vault, the Biblical writers described it according to the evidence of their senses, which is one form of accurate description. Given this dome of sky, it seemed obvious that the sun, moon and stars must be fixed to the inner side, following regular courses which it took thousands of years to work out. It is tempting to digress about ancient astronomy. To take one small sample: in Egypt, they discovered that once in every 1,260 years the dogstar Sirius rises where the sun does. This heliacal rising of Sirius, to give it its learned name, furnished the Egyptian chroniclers with a very useful epoch within which to locate their dates. But just think a minute. For at least two periods of 1,260 years, someone had been observing the sky every single night, before it was possible to verify this fact. . . . Those millennia of patient sky-watching were the greatest contribution to science of ancient times.

The dome of sky served yet another purpose. Water does not only rise up from the abyss below the earth, it comes down from above in the form of rain. Evidently then, said the ancient scientists, there must be a reservoir of some sort above the vault of heaven. And in the vault itself there must be holes through which the rain could come down. Both sources of water are mentioned in the story of the Flood: after Noe and his family were safely inside the ark, 'all the fountains of the great deep were broken up and the flood gates of heaven were opened' (Gen. 7: 11). No wonder Hebrew poets were fascinated by God's control of water!

Such is the ancient world-picture. Our first response may well be a laugh. And yet, when one thinks it over, it was a good deal to spell out, starting from nothing, with no instruments and very restricted means of travel. The tenth chapter of Genesis, known as 'The Table of Nations', gives an idea of what 'the world' meant in the days of Moses: Babylonia, Asia Minor, the Arabian Desert, Syria and Palestine, Egypt—these formed the central block. Beyond were shadowy peoples. Northwards, 'Gog' means darkness, and 'Magog' land of darkness, names applied to southern Russia. There was a similar tail-off in other directions, up the Nile, to the east, and to the west, where the Sons of Javan are probably the Ionian Greeks (Gen. 10: 2, 4).

COSMOLOGY DEVELOPS

As an account of that limited region, this ancient cosmology was as sound an interpretation of the facts as circumstances allowed. Of course, as soon as more remote regions entered the world of real experience, the picture began to be adapted. India comes in definitely with the Persian Empire, founded by Cyrus the Great, who allowed the deported Jews to return to their own land from 538 B.C. on. And by the Macchabaean period the Mediterranean lands were a good deal more definite than the 'islands' of Gen. 10: 5; Judas the Macchabee sent an embassy to Rome, and his brother Jonathan to Sparta (1 Mach. 8; 12: 1–23).

This advance in geographical knowledge naturally affected the ancient world-picture. In fact, by the time of Christ cosmology had made such important advances that the early Fathers were almost as puzzled by the ancient world-picture as we ourselves. In their days, men were asking: 'Is that round shadow on the moon at eclipses cast by a disc, a cylinder or a sphere?' That it was cast by the earth was the general educated view, but that did not decide the shape of the earth. As late as the sixteenth century a man of St. Thomas More's intellectual stature could favour the cylinder theory. It took the great navigators, Columbus, Magellan and others, to prove definitely that the earth is a sphere. As a certainty, that dates only from the sixteenth century, but as a theory the Fathers of the Church already had to cope with it.

In the providence of God, it served as a spur to make them work out a sound principle of interpretation. It is not the purpose of Holy Scripture, they concluded, to unveil to us the secrets of nature. Those we are expected to spell out for ourselves, using God's gift of reason; we are to follow in the steps of those first spellers-out whose theory, though long outmoded, gave the science of cosmology an excellent start. The Old Testament writers in fact usually describe things as they appear to the senses, such as the solid dome of the sky; beyond this, they take for granted the ideas of their times. They were not interested in the world for its own sake so much as for God's.

HEBREW ORIGINALITY

For as always, if the Jews started much where other peoples did, they took a highly original line of their own. Accounts of this cosmology in pagan sources are apt to contain details that jar on us as the Bible never does, some touches of sheer superstition, or a flat-footed literalism which never entraps the poets of the Old Testament.

Even more important, pagan peoples saw their gods as *within* the cosmos, forces operating inside the world-picture, so to speak.

Thus there was often a sky-father and an earth-mother. By contrast, the Hebrews unerringly and unswervingly saw God imaginatively as throned *above* the dome of the sky. In Ezechiel's great vision, we may remember that the cherubim carried the vault of the firmament on their wings. But outside the vault was the throne of God, and that outer side was like nothing we know on earth (see Ezech. 1: 22–8). As Isaias puts it, Heaven is God's throne, earth His footstool (Isa. 66: 1).

When Isaias had his great vision in the sanctuary of the Temple—that vision which has two echoes in the Mass—it was only God's train that filled the Temple. He Himself was above and outside the whole universe (Isa. 6: 1–13). A century and a half later, Ezechiel, writing far from the Temple, drew his imagery direct from nature as he saw it in the Euphrates valley, yet he has the same insistence. As we said above, he saw the dome of sky upheld by the wings of the cherubim, images of the great forces of nature, their power symbolised by combining characteristics of birds, animals and men. Other peoples had *kirubu* (the Babylonian form of the word) but turned them into independent deities, most impressively as anyone will know who has walked into the British Museum and met the great Babylonian bulls just inside the doors. The Jews from first to last saw these symbols of natural forces as subordinate to God, under His feet, while God's throne was outside and above the whole cosmos.

In the Apocalypse St. John uses similar imagery, with variations of his own, as every Hebrew seer did (Apoc. 4). In a sense, St. John was old fashioned, since by his day cosmology had altered a great deal. Is it fanciful to compare him to Milton, who used the Ptolemaic astronomy in *Paradise Lost*, not because he thought it better science than the Copernican but because it is more picturable? St. John, of course, was not bothering about the science of his day. Enough for him that the old cosmology survived as a picture, a fact that helps us to a right perspective on the Biblical use of such pictures.

GENESIS

The various Old Testament story-pictures are listed in the suggested reading at the end of the chapter. We need, however, to take a more careful look at the account by Moses; when all is said and done, Gen. 1: 1–2: 3 is in a class by itself. It is more reflective. It sets out to do what is done nowhere else in the Bible, give a reasonable and orderly account of how the world came to be.

What had to be said could, in a sense, be put into a single sentence: God created all that is out of nothing, and created it good. But if it had been put like that it would have gone in at one ear and out at the other. All peoples have told stories about gods that made the world, stories that even to-day appeal powerfully to the imagination, and at times are great fun. But their magnificent artistic merits were misused to put across a false view of the relation between God and the world. If the true view was to stand a chance, it must make as strong an appeal to the imagination. As much as any heathen myth it must be a work of art.

One approach is to picture Moses, bred at Pharaoh's court, educated, cultivated, abreast of all the knowledge of the day, keeping his bedouin father-in-law's sheep in the Sinai peninsula. How such a man as he came to be there can be read in the early chapters of Exodus. The desert gave him something that a court training could not, that immediate awareness of the presence of God which is all the stronger when the charm and graciousness of earth are not too much in evidence. But that immediate impact of the Divine came upon a man who could reflect upon it. That God held all in His hands was obvious in the desert. How make that truth clear to a still barbarian people, so easily beguiled by the imaginative appeal of polytheism?

It is possible that the Hebrews had brought from Mesopotamia some memory of the story of creation as told in the homeland of Abraham. More than one poem on the subject has been found, and one at least divides the action into seven stages, though they are not called 'days'. Of course Moses could have invented such a framework independently as a useful aid to memory. But as there was a real ancestral connection with Babylonia, tradition seems the more likely explanation.

After the usual Hebrew fashion, he made an independent and original use of the ideas he took over. None of these old stories for instance speak of the gods creating out of nothing; they always use some material ready to their hands. Nor have any of them any idea of God resting on the seventh day. And Moses wanted that, as the basis for the demand for the sabbath rest, by no means always a popular institution among the Hebrews. Hence his sixth day is rather crowded (verses 24–31). The land animals might well have had a whole day to themselves as the sea-creatures had done (verses 20–3), leaving the creation of man as the climax for the seventh day. But Moses' climax is the Divine rest; hence he pushes man back to the sixth day.

The strangest feature of his account is the treatment of light. Not only is the creation of sun and moon placed after the appearance of plant life, but—and this greatly puzzled the Fathers—he speaks as if there was light before the sun. Here again, a puzzle served as a providential spur to thinking out the principle of interpretation. Living among pagans, the Fathers realised, more vividly than we do, how easily mankind falls to deifying the sun. Therefore, they suggested, Moses first made clear that God is the direct Author of light; light is His creature, not an independent power of any kind. Then, as if to underline this subordinate character, he places the sun, moon and stars at a later stage.

Apart from this treatment of light, it looks as if Moses set to work to think out a reasonable order. The earth is made for man. But before man could live on it, the plants and animals needed for his food must have been there before him; and since many animals feed on plants, the plants were the earlier. And the things needed for all existence, as we know it, earth and water, those must have been in their places first.

When we go on to the second chapter of Genesis, we find this careful, reasonable order set aside. Water appears after the plants, and the animals after man. The second chapter has a quite different subject. But this totally different handling of the order of creation brings home to us that the order is not the main point of the account in either chapter. The writer uses whatever order best suits the different points he is making.

All the same, the thought-out reasonable order of the first chapter has one remarkable characteristic: it comes very close to the order worked out by modern geologists. A few things differ from the order most generally accepted, the appearance of fruit-trees, for instance. This is a valuable brake on the all-too-human tendency to think that the Bible anticipates the findings of science—fortunately for us, since those findings alter at fairly frequent intervals. Moses was not writing science. He was giving a picture, both reasonable and imaginative, to fix in the minds of his people the great truth that God made all that is, made it out of nothing, and made it good.

FOR READING

Though God's spokesmen were all along aware of the truth that God made the world, it took the discipline of the Exile in Babylon to ram it home to the consciousness of the ordinary Israelite. The Exile is a date in the assimilation of the ancient doctrine, a fact reflected in the writings of the period. The Song of the Three Children (Dan. 3: 51–90) is one expression of this new awareness, an awareness shared even by the pagan Nabuchodonosor under the influence of Daniel (Dan. 4, esp. verses 31–2). The Wisdom passage in Baruch 3: 29–35 also underlines this great lesson of the Exile.

Here then are the chief poetic pictures:

1. *Isaias*. Chapters 40: 12, 21–31; and 51: 12–16. The stress on the waters may have a practical purpose. The deportees had heard from their parents of the horrors of the desert journey on the way to Babylon, and the prophet is anxious to reassure them. See for instance 41: 14–20.

2. *Psalms*. Ps. 8; Ps. 135: 1–9. If liked, refresh your memory of Ps. 103, thought to be influenced by the *Hymn of the Sun* of the Pharaoh Akhen Aten.

3. *Proverbs* 8: 22–36. The speaker is Wisdom, here not exactly a

Divine attribute, but rather the first of created things, existing before all else, the instrument of God's action in creation.

4. *Job*. 38. If interested, read also the next three chapters, the first about the desert creatures with which Job was familiar, the next two about the far more exciting animals which the author may have seen on a visit to Egypt. Behemoth is probably the hippopotamus, though some prefer the elephant; leviathan is the crocodile.

5. *Ecclesiasticus*. There are many allusions, e.g., 17: 1–13; 18: 1–9; 24: 1–6. But the great passage is from chapter 42: 15 on to the end of 43. The author, Jesus Ben Sirach, is primarily interested in man; what he has to say of the physical world is always subordinate to his thought about the place of man in nature. Yet he has some delightful personal touches, such as his allusion to the rainbow. And like other Hebrew writers he was enchanted by frost and snow.

Here stop and try to work out for yourself the special characteristics of all these passages. Only then go on to:

6. *Genesis*. 1: 1–2: 3.

FOR DISCUSSION

1. Christians have had three main cosmologies to digest in the course of their history, that of the Old Testament, the Ptolemaic and the Copernican. And it looks as if Einstein and the physicists may be inviting us to accept yet a fourth cosmology. What help is there for us in the way the Hebrew poets had liberty in making pictures to illustrate the Biblical doctrine of creation?

2. In the seventeenth century Blaise Pascal, a scientist and astronomer, was converted to a profound personal relationship with God. His great desire was to write a book of apologetic for men who had been, like himself, thrown out of their stride, partly by the colourful worldliness of the period, but also by the Copernican astronomy. The condemnation of Galileo had given many minds a big shock. Pascal never completed the task, but on his death he left a mass of notes, published later as his *Pensées* (Thoughts). In one of these notes he makes his imaginary worried man say: 'The silence of these infinite spaces terrifies me.' It is a mistake to quote this, as is sometimes done, as if it represented Pascal's own feelings; he was too much at home in the world of science to suppose that Copernicus' cosmos was less in God's hands than Ptolemy's. But he did realise that

people with no scientific training were really shaken, feeling that Copernicus had put God much further away from them. Pascal does not seem to have written out the line of reply he would have offered. Would you like to try your hand at a line of thought to offer anyone in similar perplexity? Only, of course, to-day the perplexity would be more due to Einstein.

3. In the *Summa Contra Gentiles*, a book aimed at Mohammedans and Jews, in the thirteenth century often better scientists than Christians, St. Thomas Aquinas wrote: 'Although the hypotheses which they [the astronomers] have propounded seem to explain the facts, it does not necessarily follow that these explanations are true, for the facts about the planets may probably be explained in another way as yet unknown to men.' He was naturally thinking of the Ptolemaic astronomy, generally accepted in his age as 'the last word in science'. Try to collect together, from this book or elsewhere, all the evidence showing that Christians have often had to face challenges of this kind—a change of their world-picture without a change of their doctrine about God and the world. Then see if you can summarise the principles governing a valid response to such challenges.

CHAPTER TEN

The Life After Death

As WAS NOTICED in our second chapter, a great deal of the Old Testament was written before the Israelites came to have any clear ideas on rewards and punishments after death. Certainly they believed in survival. After death, the non-physical part, the ghost or shade, went to an underground region, a country of the dead called Sheol. But though these shades—in Hebrew the *rephaim*—continued to exist, everything that gave life savour and meaning had come to an end. All distinctions, of rich and poor, subject and ruler, oppressor and oppressed, even of good or bad, were done away. The only thing one could say of Sheol was that NOTHING with which we are familiar on earth could happen there.

Yet that Nothing proves on closer inspection to be a very big Something. We see this best by considering the ideas of other peoples. Both the Greek Hades and the Babylonian Arallu are, like Sheol, an underworld where differences ceased and the ghosts lived a life emptied of all meaning. Yet even the Greeks and the Babylonians projected some odds and ends of human experience into the underworld life of the dead. They did not do this on as big a scale as a people whose beliefs were superior to theirs, in some ways superior even to the original Hebrew belief. Of all the peoples of the ancient world, the Egyptians are outstanding in the extent to which they got hold of the truth that our fate after death is conditioned by our conduct on earth.

And now comes the astonishing thing. In spite of this important superiority, the Egyptians did on a big scale what practically all peoples have done on some scale: they projected their experiences on earth into the world of the dead. That is what the tomb-paintings of Egypt are all about. In the next world, a ghost needed the ghosts of all the things he had had on earth, ghost-food, ghost-houses and furniture, ghost-servants, even ghost-hunting and ghost-dancing-girls in the case of the wealthy. The pictures were a way of conveying these necessities to the world of the dead. Another highly civilised people, the Chinese, used to burn paper models of houses, furniture, and so forth, with the same idea: to provide the dead with the things they needed.

HEBREW SPECIALITIES

By contrast, the Hebrews are found insisting that the life of the dead is NOT LIKE THE LIFE OF THE LIVING ON EARTH. A Hebrew could give quite a long list of what the dead don't do; but not once in the Old Testament are we given a hint of what they do do. That was an astonishing feat, genuinely unique. No one else managed to keep their conception of the life after death wholly negative. In a vividly imaginative people, as the Hebrews were, it is particularly astonishing.

Further, this firm sticking to the negative was far from a negative achievement. It provided a positive growing-point, because, while much further growth was needed, no false growths needed to be cleared away. Everything in the Hebrew conception was a genuine seed which, in God's good time, could grow without getting choked by a wild undergrowth of falsehoods.

There are other differences. Nearly everywhere in the world there has been a feeling that the ghosts cannot go where they belong unless helped by special rites. If there was no one to perform the rites, then the ghost had no resource but to hang around making a nuisance of himself to the living. Then too, making offerings to the dead is almost world-wide, not limited to the Egyptians and Chinese. But when the Israelites for once did it, it was remembered for centuries as a particular horror of wickedness (Ps. 105: 28, referring back to the ugly incident recorded in Num. 25: 1–5). The Babylonians, whose ideas on the underworld were closest to the Hebrew—not surprising since Abraham came from Mesopotamia—believed that a ghost who had no one to offer food for him was reduced to eating the leavings of slightly luckier ghosts. There is no trace of such ideas among the Hebrews, except as a result of contamination by the surrounding peoples, as at Beel Phegor.

Another practice highly developed among neighbouring peoples was necromancy. This was absolutely forbidden in the Law of Moses, though at times the Israelites fell away from their own faith and practice (Lev. 19: 31; 20: 6 and 27; Deut. 18: 10–12; 4 Kings 21: 6; Isa. 8: 19). In the story of Saul and the witch of Endor, it is commonly held that though the woman called up something more than she had bargained for, it was not the spirit of Samuel (1 Kings 28). Genuine cases of raising the dead are never spoken of as returns from Sheol (4 Kings 4: 8–37 for instance). To come back from Sheol meant to recover from near-fatal illness or to escape death at the hands of enemies.

There is one even greater difference. All other nations thought of the underworld of the dead as having its own gods or rulers, Dis, Pluto, Osiris, and so forth. Only once in the Bible is such a thing suggested, and it is definitely a piece of 'local colour', so strange that translators generally tone it down. The author of the Book of Job chose as his hero an Edomite who had lived long ago when the descendants of Jacob's brother Esau were still monotheists. He is very careful not to foist on Job and his friends ideas and rites that were special to the Jews. In speaking of Sheol he keeps to the common stock of ideas among the Semitic peoples. Hence he gives Sheol some sort of ruler of its own, perhaps not exactly a god, but definitely its own guardian spirit, called in Hebrew 'the king of terrors' (Job 18: 14). In all other books of the Old Testament, when Hebrews are talking among themselves, so to speak, it is made clear that the ruler of Sheol is Yahweh Himself (Ps. 138: 8; Prov. 15: 11).

HOW THE LIVING LOOKED AT THINGS

We start then from the fact that the Hebrews began with a few very simple ideas, all true, but, as we now know, incomplete. They knew that the spiritual part of man survives death. They knew that death is a leveller. They held fast to the truth that the life after death is unlike the life on earth, save in one particular: the dead too are under the rule of the One God. It does not sound much, but it is all good, clean seed.

In prose passages the name Sheol is regularly used; unfortunately it is often translated 'hell', which is confusing. Sheol was something distinct from the literal tomb (Gen. 37: 35, where hell means Sheol). But in poetry, the parallelism of Hebrew verse brought into use a wide range of synonyms. Sheol is called darkness, silence, a pit or hole, corruption, destruction (in Hebrew *abaddon*). It is the land from which none returns, hence it is insatiable, yearning (yawning) for its prey, the image of those who can never have enough.

Of course the idea of reward and punishment was not absent from Hebrew religion, but it operated in this life. Further, the unit of moral responsibility was the community rather than the individual. The nearest thing to immortality for an individual was to have children; it was in his descendants that his life on earth was continued. Hence though it was considered normal for a good man to have a long life and plenty of children, he and they might be involved in a calamity which the evil-doing community had brought upon itself. If God did not intervene to save a good man in such a case, he had no grounds for complaint. The way in which God would make it up to him would be to secure him a worthy posterity.

SHOCKS TO THE OLD IDEAS

That is roughly the attitude from which the Israelites started. What first gave it a shake was the oppression of the poor of which we read in Amos and Osee and later. If Israel was oppressed by foreign enemies, it was because God's people had forsaken His Law and broken its side of the Covenant made on Mount Sinai. But when bad rich Israelites began to oppress good poor ones, the old confidence was challenged in a new way. That was the first shock. The second came when the doom pronounced on God's disobedient people was fulfilled, for the instruments of that doom, Assyrians and Babylonians, were more wicked than the Chosen People themselves. Clearly, the old view no longer squared with the observed facts of life. A remarkably large part of the Old Testament is given over to thrashing out the issues thus raised.

Further, as the prophets developed the idea of the Messianic Age, an idea closely associated with the promises of a Return from Exile, it looks as if people began to say: 'That's all very fine for those who will be alive then, but what about us? What's the point of serving God now if we are merely to be swallowed up by Sheol before the Age of Messias? And what about all those who served God faithfully in times past? Does being born in a particular period make as big a difference as all that? . . .' So from three sides this issue of faithful service to God pushed to the front the inadequacies in the conception of Sheol.

THE RESURRECTION OF THE BODY

In the later books of the Old Testament—parts of Daniel, Macchabees, Wisdom—we find that the best Israelites had come to believe in the resurrection of the body. It was the whole man, body as well as soul, who had served God. Hence it would be the whole man, body as well as soul, who would be recalled to share in the age of peace and joy ushered in by the Messias. No other people arrived at this conclusion. It is the most unique element in the final Jewish solution. Indeed, the Book of Wisdom makes this belief in the resurrection of the body the dividing line between good and bad in Israel.

And yet, when we try to trace out the process by which the Jews arrived at this remarkable conclusion we run unto difficulties. It is true that from about the time of Isaias onwards various writers, both of Prophetic and of Wisdom books, use language which to our Christian ears seems to refer to belief in a resurrection—so much so that translations sometimes make the reference sound more definite than it actually is. For closer study, especially in Hebrew, makes it apparent that what was in mind was a resurgence of the whole nation. Captivity and

Exile are described as death, and the reconstitution of the nation as a rising from that death. A familiar instance is the *De Profundis*, which expresses Israel's attitude while undergoing this 'death' of captivity.

Now perhaps we can more easily understand something at first sight rather curious: right down to the time of Christ an important party among the Jews refused to believe in the resurrection of the body. True, the Sadducees were the more worldly, unspiritual section of the nation. But when Our Lord answered their challenge, He did not draw on any of the prophetic or wisdom passages which at first sight seem to refer to a rising from the dead. He went back behind the whole of later Hebrew thought to the God of Abraham, of Isaac, and of Jacob.

Early Christian writers, however, from St. Paul onwards, often used these passages referring to the resurgence of the captive nation when they were speaking of the resurrection of the body. The beautiful metaphors of the ancient prophets were so often the most apt phrases to use of the truth now known with absolute certainty through Christ. Indeed, we may perhaps feel that the Holy Ghost had inspired those old wrestlers with truth to use phrases relevant to their own immediate situation and hopes, but which were also echoes in advance of further and deeper truths. Certainly Christian translators of the Old Testament have tended to render these passages concerning national resurgence in a way that makes our thoughts fly to the resurrection of the just.

For—and here is a point of great importance—the Jews were far more concerned with the fate of the just than of the wicked. They were astonishingly free from any kind of vengefulness. For centuries, it was enough for them that the wicked should go down to the meaningless life of Sheol, losing the fruits that their evil-doing had apparently won for them. In the Old Testament, the wrestle is almost wholly about the fate of the good.

GOD'S GUIDANCE

When we survey the whole course, one of the strangest features at first sight is that God gave His people so little direct help. Prophet after prophet protested to God about the injustices of this world, yet God does not say: 'It will all be squared up after death'. He says in effect, 'You have Me. What more do you want?' Which is in one way the only complete answer, yet in another feels to the protestor like missing all his real points.

It is genuinely strange. And yet, as we go on watching, another impression gains ground. Secretly and in the background, God must have given simply enormous help, keeping His people from rushing off down roads that other peoples tried and found to be dead-ends. Above all, God kept them from the disastrous blunder of reading their earthly experience into the life of the dead in Sheol.

And yet, in a way, that answer, 'You have Me', was like turning a knife in a wound. Yahweh was indeed the ruler of Sheol. But His relations with the shades were utterly unlike His relations with His servants on earth. Since nothing ever happened in Sheol, there was no room for God's providence, nothing to pray about, nothing to thank Him for. And the greatest joy of choice souls, the worship in the Temple, would come to an end like every other human activity. When we try to follow the good Israelite in his mental anguish before the thought of death, we receive perhaps the sharpest jolt of our whole exploration: The cruellest pang of death was that there would be in Sheol no such intimacy with God as had been enjoyed on earth. What are we to say about people whose chief protest at death was that they would no longer be able to praise God (Ps. 113: 25)? While there were other complaints, this was the heart and centre of their anguish. . . . And yet, it was this very anguish that kept them on the right path, for the only answer to it is the Beatific Vision.

This passionate attachment to God and longing for His Presence explains what at first may seem strange, the way the

Jews at first reacted unfavourably to Greek speculations on immortality. True, at first they met those speculations in a very inferior form, nothing like the great thoughts of Socrates and Plato. In Egypt, which was the Jewish point of contact with Hellenism, they met men arguing that since spirit is the 'lightest' thing that is, the soul, being a spirit, must 'rise upwards' when at death it is freed from the body. There is more at stake here than the fact that a Jew was accustomed to thinking of the shades going 'down' to Sheol. Though no Jew seems to have put his finger on the point, this conception of 'spirit' is still materialistic. The Jew by-passed that because he saw at once that there was here no answer to the cry of his heart, no indication that death would keep him in the presence of God. If God were absent, what did it matter whether souls went 'up' or 'down'? The distinction was utterly irrelevant and boring (Eccles. 3: 21).

And as a matter of fact, even the truly philosophic and spiritual conception of immortality which we owe to the great Greek philosophers tends even now to strike many people as thin and off the point; it does not give them what they instinctively want; they are not going to waste time over it. . . . All the same, the Ecclesiast, jotting down his thoughts as his life passed on, did at last begin to see a possible strand of sense in the Greek speculations: the body would return to dust, the spirit to God who gave it (Eccles. 12: 7). This later jotting in his notebook dodges the materialism which jars in the type of Greek speculation he had earlier rejected. Man is made to the image of God. The idea that the soul has some kind of affinity with Him is, after all, important.

THE LAST STAGES

Only in the latest books of the Old Testament do we arrive at anything like a clear insight into the life after death—and quite possibly we Christians, inheriting a much fuller and more rounded view, may chiefly feel its incompleteness. We never pass entirely out of the realm of wrestle, discussion, even agony, which was tied up with the question of the Innocent Sufferer. Only by degrees was it seen that the two problems, the life after death and the suffering of the innocent, could not be fruitfully considered apart. Incidentally, neither is a purely intellectual or academic problem, something from which we can stand back in safe superiority while we work out our sum. Both are not only moral problems, but problems of anguished hearts, indeed of anguished flesh and blood.

By very slow degrees the Jews did come to see that the only solution in the case of the Good Poor Man—their expression for the innocent sufferer—was a reward after death. And since the only reward that such a man would have any use for was the Presence of God Himself, the reward was not something external, artificially added on. It was the man's own goodness coming to its final bloom according to its own inward character, still more according to the character of God who had sustained him in all his sufferings and bewilderment. To hold on to: 'You have Me—what more do you want?' when everything seemed against God, that was the true preparation for having the only thing he really wanted: God Himself.

It was only when they were arriving at this point that the Jews began to see that the wicked similarly reached their own natural fruition, separation from God. It is the pain of loss which the author of the Book of Wisdom stresses. Just and unjust would arise from the dead, the just to enjoy for ever the Presence of God, the unjust to suffer the absence from Him. In each case the result was the one which grew out of their own choices, the character each had formed for himself.

The whole long story is recapitulated for us by St. John: 'Dearly beloved, we are now the sons of God: and it hath not appeared what we shall be. We know that, when He shall appear, we shall be like Him, because we shall see Him as He is' (1 John 3: 2). Here, neither 'survival' nor 'immortality' is the right word. The Macchabaean martyrs talk of it as 'new life' or 'eternal life'. Our Lord often calls it simply 'life', as if nothing else deserves the word—as indeed it does not. But He sometimes particularises, speaking of 'eternal life' or 'life more abundant'. We are not fobbed off with a mere continuance of existence (survival), nor even with the fact that our souls are by nature incapable of death (immortality). What we have to look forward to is a new kind of life, a reflection of, indeed a participation in, the life of God Himself. . . . But for the final stages we have to wait for the New Testament.

FOR READING

1. *Where the Jews started from.* Job 3: 11–19; Isa. 14: 4–21 (in verse 9 the 'giants' are the rephaim, the shades); Ezech. 32, esp. verses 17–22; Assur is Assyria; Ps. 87.

2. *The Resurgence of the Nation.* While the following passages do not refer directly to the resurrection of the just, they furnished some of the language later used when that belief came to be definitely held: Isa. 26: 13–21; Ezech. 37: 1–14.

3. *The Final Stage.* Dan. 12: 2. (The vision section of Daniel deals with the Macchabaean period and may have been written then, an example of pseudepigraphy: See Introduction, p. 5.)

The Macchabaean martyrs: Eleazar, 2 Mac. 6: 18–31; the seven brothers and their mother, chapter 7. The mother is notable, not only for her heroic support of her sons, but for the highly individual reasons she gives for her faith. Prayers for the dead; chap. 12: 38–46.

4. *The Book of Wisdom.* This is probably somewhat earlier than the time of the Macchabees, and shows a Jew in Egypt thinking out in times of quiet the issues for which the martyrs later died. The author regards belief in the resurrection as the line dividing the just from the unjust. The chief passage is chapter 1: 12 to the end of chapter 3; chapters 4 and 5 continue the theme. Chapter 5 is a remarkable analysis of the barren attitude called *remorse*, regret on realising that wrong-doing has not paid, but without sorrow for the sin itself. Shakespeare's *Macbeth* is a full-length study of remorse; there is not a word of repentance in the whole play. In the Book of Wisdom, the punishment in view is the pain of loss.

FOR DISCUSSION

Perhaps our best course is to consider the subject from the standpoint of our post-Christian friends. What we have read in the Old Testament has surely awakened a hope that this pre-Christian wrestle with the challenge of our lot on earth has priceless help to give in handling their problems with sympathy and understanding. One difficulty apt to be met is that our friends are liable to dismiss Christian beliefs as a ready-made, parrot-like solution reached by running away from the harsh facts of life. The story of this wrestle by those for whom life was often exceedingly harsh might, handled rightly, persuade our friends to reconsider.

1. Among the ideas at the back of many minds to-day is that belief in hell is a cheap way of getting even with enemies too strong for us here on earth. Yet those who thrashed out the problems of the life after death were concerned primarily for the fate of the good, those who sincerely loved God, and only arrived half-accidentally at the punishment of the wicked.

2. It is not uncommon to find people claiming that we can live a good life on earth without the sanction of rewards and punishments after death, and that this kind of goodness is the only one that is genuinely disinterested. How does the Old Testament help us to sort out what is right and what is muddle-headed in this notion?

3. What help have we here in getting people to see that everything turns on the question they are asking? A wrong question can never issue in a right answer. Instead of arguing with our friends about their answers, would it not be better to challenge them about their questions? What are we all asking of reality, for instance? That it shall confound good and bad together? That it shall show obvious favouritism for the good here on earth, or what?

4. There is also the question of the kind of reality they have in mind. Is it impersonal, like the impersonal moral order that underlies the Hindu doctrine of reincarnation? Or is it a personal reality like the God of Jews and Christians? The impersonal reality is no good to them if their chief concern is to meet again those they loved on earth. But a personal reality is bound to make personal demands on us. It cannot be accountable to us; we are accountable to It—or rather, to Him—no matter how dark or inscrutable It (He) may seem. Not everyone is ready to face this challenge of the personal reality.

Selected Dates in Old Testament History

Note on Dating. Our present all but exact solar calendar has only been in use for a little over a century and a half. This fact may enable us to sympathise with those who have had to work out the dates in periods when the solar calendar was only in process of formation, in the history of peoples whose methods of dating often differed widely. Given the difficulties, remarkable success has been attained, but not absolute certainty. Only where there are astronomical data—comets, eclipses and so forth—can we be sure that something happened in one definite year.

1. All peoples began with a lunar calendar, which may still survive as a religious calendar—we ourselves still date Easter by the moon. Only when mankind began to grow crops did it become necessary to know exactly the right time to sow the seed. The quest for an accurate solar calendar is the quest for the right time for sowing.

2. Even when peoples had worked out a calendar of twelve months of thirty days each, giving a year of 360 days, it was only a few years till seeds began to be sown dangerously early. Peoples varied in the devices used for overcoming this difficulty. The Egyptians, for instance, added five extra intercalary days before their new year. But even so, seedtime after a while began to come too early.

3. There were different methods of dating a reign. The Jews counted part-years as whole years—just as they counted part-days as whole days. Christ's body lay in the tomb part of Friday, all of Saturday and part of Sunday, making three days by Jewish reckoning. Similarly, if a king reigned from (let us say) December to January twelvemonth, he could be said to have reigned three years. The Babylonians, however, would have said he reigned for two years, as they counted from the first New Year's Day after his accession. Both methods of reckoning are used in the Old Testament. Further, New Year's Day was not the same everywhere; some Old Testament writers use the Jewish year, some the Persian, some the Greek.

4. The greatest difficulty of all was that there was no generally

accepted year from which to reckon. We count backwards from the Birth of Christ, but those who lived before Him naturally did not.

Given the difficulties, scholars have arrived at remarkable results. But they do not all agree in all details. Broadly, dating becomes markedly more exact from about the time of Solomon onwards. As the details do not concern a book of this type, this book follows, with a very few exceptions, the chronology given in para. 125g of *A Catholic Commentary on Holy Scripture*, (published by Thos. Nelson & Sons).

I. THE LATE BRONZE AGE

Bible History	*World History*
	c. 1780 B.C. A Semitic dynasty, the Hyksos, establishes itself in Egypt.
c. 1750 B.C. Abraham goes from Mesopotamia to Chanaan as part of a wave of Semitic emigrants.	
c. 1700 B.C. Jacob goes down into Egypt—where Joseph is already established as Grand Vizier under the Hyksos.	
	c. 1550 B.C. A native Egyptian dynasty drives out the Hyksos. The Israelites are unpopular because they had been protégés of the fallen regime.
The 15th century B.C. One possible period for the Exodus.	
	c. 1375 B.C. Akhen Aten comes to the throne, the Pharaoh who composed the *Hymn of the Sun.*
The 13th century B.C. A more probable period for the Exodus.	

II. THE EARLY IRON AGE

Bible History	*World History*
	Before 1200 B.C. The Aramaeans (Syrians) drive out the Chanaanites from east of Lebanon. Their chief kingdom makes its capital at Damascus.
c. 1250 B.C. The Israelites under Josue enter Chanaan from the east.	*c.* 1200 B.C. The Philistines enter Chanaan from the sea.
1250–1050 B.C. The approximate period of the Judges.	
	c. 1150 B.C. The Philistines try to conquer the central plateau occupied by the Israelites, who set up a monarchy to secure united action.

III. THE UNITED MONARCHY

c. 1050–1012. Reign of Saul.

c. 1012–972. Reign of David.

c. 972–931. Reign of Solomon.

IV. THE DIVIDED MONARCHY—SELECTED DATES ONLY

Dating now becomes much more exact

Kingdom of Juda	*Kingdom of Israel*	*World Affairs*
931–913 B.C. Roboam	931–910 B.C. Jeroboam I with Egyptian support sets up a separate kingdom consisting of the ten Northern Tribes.	
	884–853 B.C. Achab.	853 B.C. Battle of Karkar (or Qarqar). The Assyrians defeat the small countries of Western Asia. Achab loses all his chariots and a body of infantry.
	Period of Elias and later of Eliseus.	
	841–814 B.C. Jehu, a usurper, founds a new dynasty.	841 B.C. Jehu pays tribute to Shalmaneser III of Assyria.
	782–753 B.C. Jeroboam II, great-grandson of Jehu.	
		Israel begins to be aware of Assyria as more than a temporary menace.
768–740 B.C. Azarias or Ozias, a great king, but stricken with leprosy for his presumption in offering incense in the Temple.		
740 B.C. Call of Isaias (Isa. 6).		
740–735 B.C. Joatham.		Assyria presses as far south as Israel.
736–727 B.C. Achaz, who paid tribute to Assyria.		
	730–721 B.C. Osee (not the prophet) the last king of Israel, appointed by the Assyrians.	
		724 B.C. Samaria besieged by the Assyrians under Shalmaneser V.
		721 B.C. Samaria taken by the Assyrians under Sargon II.
	721 B.C. Samaria destroyed and the Ten Tribes deported.	
	End of the Kingdom of Israel.	

V. THE KINGDOM OF JUDA ALONE

727–698 B.C. Ezechias, the reforming king. Isaias at the height of his influence.

705–681 B.C. Reign of Sennacherib of Assyria.

701 B.C. Sennacherib comes south to punish the revolt against him. Juda is slightly involved, but Jerusalem is saved from capture, though Ezechias has to pay a huge tribute.

698–643 B.C. Manasses, in whose reign Isaias is thought to have been murdered.

641–609 B.C. Josias, a reforming king.

628 B.C. Call of Jeremias.

625 B.C. A Chaldean dynasty captures Babylon.

612 B.C. Capture and destruction of Nineve, the Assyrian capital, by Chaldaeans and allies, under the lead of the Chaldaean crown prince Nabuchodonosor.

609 B.C. Pharao Nechao goes to the help of Assyria. At Megiddo he defeats and kills King Josias of Juda.

609 B.C. Joachaz, the popular choice, deposed and deported by Pharao Nechao, who appoints instead:

609–598 B.C. Joachim or Joakim.

605 B.C. Crown prince Nabuchodonosor defeats combined Egyptians and Assyrians at Carchemish. Pursues them south and takes from Joachim a number of boys for his service, one of them being Daniel. The *First Deportation* to Babylon. Nabuchodonosor returns to Babylon on news of his accession.

598 B.C. Joachim foolishly revolts against Babylon, but dies before vengeance overtakes him, leaving his son

598 B.C. Joachin or Jechonias to face the storm after a reign of only three months.

598 B.C. Nebuchodonosor comes south to punish the revolt. Deposes Joachin, and deports him with many notables. The *Second Deportation* which included Ezechiel.

598–586 B.C. Sedecias, appointed king as nominee of Babylon. He took a special oath of allegiance, but broke it.

587 B.C. Nebuchodonosor lays siege to Jerusalem.

586 B.C. Jerusalem taken; city and Temple destroyed. *Third Deportation*, generally called the Exile to Babylon.

End of the Kingdom of Juda

VI. PERSIAN PERIOD

539 B.C. Babylon besieged by Cyrus the Great of Persia.

538 B.C. Babylon taken by Cyrus.

538 B.C. Decree of Cyrus permitting the Jews to return to their own land. First Return. Building of Second Temple begun.

515 B.C. Dedication of the Temple.

458 B.C. Return under Esdras.

445 B.C. Nehemias appointed governor of Jerusalem by the Persians.

333 B.C. Persians overthrown by Alexander the Great.

VII. GREEK PERIOD

323 B.C. Death of Alexander the Great. His generals divide up his empire. At first Juda belonged in the region ruled from Egypt by the Ptolemy dynasty, but later was taken from Egypt and incorporated in the Seleucid Empire, founded by another of Alexander's generals, with its capital at Antioch in Syria.

175 B.C. Antiochus IV called Epiphanes (the Illustrious) usurps the throne at Antioch and sets out to Hellenise all his dominions.

167 B.C. Antiochus sets up his image in the Temple at Jerusalem ('the Abomination of desolation' spoken of by the prophet).

166 B.C. Revolt of a priestly family led by the father Mathathias. He was soon killed and his son *Judas the Macchabee* took the lead.

164 B.C. Temple purified, commemorated by the Feast of the Purification.
This revolt went on, led by one after another of the Macchabee brothers, until 135 B.C.

135 B.C. John Hyrcanus founds the Asmonaean dynasty, which ruled in Juda until the rise of Herod the Great.